Teaching Your Children Photography

Teaching Your Children Photography:

A Step-by-Step Guide

Don Cyr

AMPHOTO

American Photographic Book Publishing Co., Inc.

Garden City, New York

Dedicated to Joan

Published in Garden City, New York, by American Photographic Book Publishing Co., Inc. All rights reserved. No part of this book may be reproduced in any form without the written consent of the publisher.

Library of Congress Catalog Card No.: 77-72291

ISBN: 0-8174-0597-6 (hardbound)
ISBN: 0-8174-2416-4 (softbound)

Manufactured in the United States of America.

Contents

Foreword

Today, there is a growing awareness among teachers, parents, and school administrators that photography belongs in the classroom, and at an early stage of the educational process. Photography's value has been widely appreciated by teachers who have used it as a way of helping children relate creatively with the world and other people, as a means of self-realization, and as an exciting adjunct to the teaching of literature, history, social sciences, and other subjects. What has been lacking is good basic "how to" information on starting photographic programs for grade school youngsters. This book by Professor Don Cyr is a valuable contribution to filling that gap.

My first contact with Don came some time after participating in a symposium of educators, psychologists, and teachers on "Photography as a Fourth R," sponsored in July 1975 by **Popular Photography** magazine. Although the distinguished specialists on the panel were generally enthusiastic about the idea of adding photography to the grade school curriculum, many were skeptical or pessimistic about the possibilities of this ever happening on a wide scale. The problems, and they continue to be real ones, include tight school budgets, lack of understanding by parents and school administrators as to the value of photography, lack of rigorous research to support the subjective evaluations of teachers who have used photography successfully, and, very important, lack of photographic training and knowledge among teachers themselves. It was in this last area that it seemed to me **Popular Photography** could perform a useful service, and that Don Cyr was the ideal person to be involved.

Don's warmth and enthusiasm are contagious, his imagination in devising exciting, inexpensive projects is remarkable, and his advice is based on first-hand classroom experience. The nucleus of what later became a ten-part magazine series, "How to Turn Your Kid on to Photography," and now considerably expanded to become this book, was a program Don developed with fourth-grade classes in Madison, Connecticut, with joint funding from the National Endowment for the Arts, the "Visiting Artists Program" of the Connecticut Commission on the Arts, and the Madison township.

The series of ten projects published in **Popular Photography** stimulated much enthusiastic response from teachers, educators, and other adults working with youngsters. A high point was a one-day seminar/workshop, "Simple Photography in Your Classroom," sponsored by **Popular Photography** at the New School for Social Research in New York for about 100 grade school teachers. The heart of the workshop sessions involved actually doing four of Don's projects. The teachers loved it and gave all concerned a standing ovation at the wrap-up session. One could only hope that later on the kids in their classrooms had even half as much fun as the teachers themselves did that day.

Don's projects **are** fun. They are relatively simple and provide feedback, which is obviously important when you're involved with young children, but they also offer wide scope for creativity. Also, many of them are quite inexpensive, involving cameraless photography or the use of low-cost disposable equipment. And they are adaptable to many contexts and special needs. I can't imagine any creative grade school teacher looking through this book without finding a number of projects that could be utilized in his or her classroom.

In an increasingly complex environment, our children need all the visual expertise and sophistication we can help them acquire. The simple but delightful projects in this book should get things off to a productive start.

Arthur Goldsmith
Editorial Director
Popular Photography

Preface

How often have you really wanted to turn your kid on to photography, but decided not to for one reason or another? Well, you're not alone; it's a trek that each of us has wanted to make now and then. Nobody has to tell us how exciting photography is. We know that, or we wouldn't be so wrapped up in the medium ourselves. Still, for one reason or another, be it cost, lack of time or the proper space, or just plain "How do I begin?", we've never really started teaching that child photography.

Of course, we're not about to let that kid of ours run around loose with one of our expensive 35mm single-lens reflex cameras, and we're not particularly enthusiastic about sharing our costly darkroom equipment either. Nevertheless, if you're like me, you'd like to turn your kid on to photography. We know what it's done for us! Once you get hooked, there's no way to kick the habit. And who wants to, anyway?

The world we see through the viewfinder of a camera is a very special world; it's **our** world. It's not always the best of worlds, but for some reason it seems to be so much more palatable when we look at it through that little peephole in the back of a camera. For some obscure reason, photography seems to make the rest of life much more coherent. Shouldn't we share this with our kids?

Even if we aren't particularly concerned about the therapeutic aspects of the medium, can we afford to neglect the communications point of view? In a world where better communications may be our only salvation, we can no longer tolerate either verbal or **visual** illiteracy. Today, the majority of people in this country achieve verbal literacy. Yet with global television in the midst of our lives, why is the pressing need to learn the visual language not being recognized as a valid educational goal by those who are in a position to make the necessary changes?

The world around us is continually being woven into one immense visual/verbal fabric. Images are the warp and words are the weft of the gigantic societal tapestry into which each of us is inextricably woven. The image and the word comprise the very foundation of our cultural integration. And yet, too few of our schools teach photography to children or include any aspect of learning the visual language in their respective programs. We see reading being taught as if imagery were superfluous to understanding!

The proper utilization of photography in the schools could possibly revolutionize our fundamental attitudes to-ward education. Though photography is not a panacea for the educational ills that exist, it is as essential to the proper education of a child as reading, writing, and arithmetic. If photography ever ascends to its rightful place in the curriculum, right beside the three R's, children will have at their disposal one of the most powerful learning tools ever created. Let us hope that the teaching of the visual language through photography catches on soon. The need is obvious; the potential is limitless.

In the meantime, parents and teachers who are into photography just can't wait any longer for society or the educational community to recognize the values inherent in teaching photography to children. We must act now! We can't allow today's kids to grow up without knowing at least the basics of photography. Tomorrow's grown-ups need every tool they can get their hands on to cope with the future. Let's face it: The camera, like the typewriter and the pocket calculator, is here to stay. Images, words, and numbers—that's where our world is at. Since we can depend on our schools to pump words and numbers into our kids, why don't **we** accept the task of providing them with an opportunity to turn on to the world of images by teaching them photography?

The main purpose of this book is to help furnish the reader with the basics of a photography program designed especially for children. The materials and techniques of photography that are covered will require a minimum of hardware, be most economical, take very little time, and also be suitable for practically any situation. In the last section entitled "Sources and Resources," you will find a listing of all the materials needed for the projects and where they can be purchased, in addition to audiovisual aids, books, and other publications that will prove to be most helpful.

Beginning with several projects in cameraless photography, the series will progress through the fundamentals of pinhole photography on into the more inexpensive and budget-priced cameras that any child can use. Setting up temporary darkrooms and doing some basic darkroom experimentation are also included. The emphasis is placed on producing good images without expensive equipment in your bathroom, kitchen, or, for that matter, wherever you can temporarily arrange the few accessories necessary for the project.

To begin with, we may have to modify some of our attitudes toward working with the medium before we can start teaching that kid photography. The whole emphasis of this book is directed toward turning kids on to images, not necessarily techniques. The assumption is that if a child really enjoys making images, he or she will seek to improve the technical proficiency needed to produce even better images. Consequently, we don't want to run the risk of turning the child off by making the techniques of image production too overwhelming. Readiness is the key factor. The child should not be given any more information than can be readily assimilated and verified by virtue of the image results that he himself can readily achieve.

All processing of photomaterials should be greatly curtailed to achieve the most immediate results with a minimum of effort. For example (and here I may be preaching blasphemy), we must not overemphasize print permanency with children. So what if the kid's work is not processed to archival standards—he or she may lose or misplace the picture within a couple of days anyway. It's the experience that counts, not the product! We want children to enjoy making images. We don't want them to be unnecessarily concerned about preserving the images for posterity. Therefore, the techniques of photography should be customized to fit the circumstances of learning. It is very important at this point to mention that learning photography should be just plain fun for the child. If either the child or the parent is not up to par for a project in photography, it should be postponed. There should be no sense of urgency or duty involved in teaching a child photography. It should be an enjoyable activity from start to finish for all the parties concerned.

People who have been into photography for some time tend to be very critical of images, their own included. This is a very important aspect of serious photography study, **but not with children.** Critical judgments on the part of the person doing the teaching should be reserved for the more advanced stages of photographic study. When you are working with youngsters, criticism should be eliminated, and all judgments should be reserved to "Keep up the good work, Johnny."

If getting the child all fired up about photography is our main goal, then approval is the only big stick we should carry. What we must do is try to encourage the child to explore the potentialities of the medium as it relates to his particular vision. Since we're concerned mainly with teaching the image-making possibilities of the medium, the tenor of the explorations that we encourage should be geared to furthering the child's own understandings of the world around him.

Each child is an individual and must be guided to the discovery of his own inner capacity. Children should not be molded into our own image or shaped to conform to our particular ideas of what should be. We must be wary of foisting our personal way of seeing on the unsuspecting child.

Children learn more from what we do than from what we say. The quality of our relationship with children greatly affects the degree to which they accept or reject our instruction. We must watch how we respond to children and how we interact with them. Children respond more to the parent's or teacher's attitude than to anything else. They learn less from our words than they do from our nonverbal expressions and the manner in which we react to them. If we as teachers or parents create an atmosphere of relaxed approval, the child will feel free to explore the natural interrelationships that exist between vision and the environment.

Make photography a meaningful part of life itself. Children are more aware of the here and now and more in tune with it than most adults. As they grow up, they too learn to **tune out**—a sheer survival mechanism in today's world. If we try, we can help children keep the childlike vision that so many adult artist/photographers seem to reclaim only after many years of search and hard work.

Children accept rules and live up to them more easily and faithfully when they understand the "why" of each rule. Encouraging children to express themselves does not necessitate permissiveness. Children both need and welcome specific do's and don'ts. Process and technique are important to successful photography. Discipline in any art form is essential, and it should be insisted upon right from the start. If you take a laissez-faire approach, you might as well forget about teaching photography to kids.

The child's overall success depends upon his ability to follow the directions necessary to carry out the procedures involved. Insist upon adherence to certain rules. These rules must be strict enough to produce the desired product, but loose enough to allow each child room to grow and learn from the experience.

Keep the channels of communication open. A good self-image is essential to psychological growth. We can foster this by making communication a two-way process. As teachers or parents of children, we need to listen to them, to keep tuned in so we can give the right kind of help that is needed and not just another put-down.

Actually, **encouragement and praise cannot be overemphasized.** They are a must, no matter what the results. There is always another chance to make images. The process may fail, but the experience of trial and error is the real challenge. As long as children begin to realize that life includes success as well as failure, they will be better prepared for adult living where life isn't always easy or successful.

Don Cyr
Cheshire, Connecticut

Project 1:

Sun Pictures

Photograms are created by placing a few objects on a piece of photosensitive paper, exposing the arrangement to a light source, and subsequently processing the paper in the proper chemicals to obtain the final product. To carry out this operation, some sort of darkroom is essential. Making sungrams, however, offers the same experience, but without the need for the usual darkroom paraphernalia.

Instead of using the customary photoenlarging paper, a special printing paper called printing-out paper (P.O.P.) is employed. This paper has definite advantages: It can be handled under normal room light and it requires no developer. Hence, the need for a darkroom is eliminated, and chemicals are unnecessary. Any room, anywhere, can become a photographic workshop.

Printing-out paper is produced by several different photographic manufacturers, each paper under its own respective brand name. One of the most readily available types of P.O.P. is Kodak's Studio Proof F. Do not purchase Kodak's Portrait Proof R; it requires the use of a developer.

Studio Proof F produces a purplish-brown image when it is exposed to sunlight or other forms of ultraviolet illumination, such as a sunlamp. The image darkens in relation to the length of time the paper is exposed to light. Development of the paper occurs as if by magic. Anything from weeds to toy soldiers can be exposed on this paper to produce an image.

By placing on opaque object on the paper and exposing the paper to sunlight or bright daylight, a silhouette of the object will result. Images produced in this manner provide a fascinating and exciting experience for children; they can actually observe the changes that take place. The entire process takes about three to six minutes, depending on light conditions. The purplish-brown images that result, however, do eventually fade away.

After the opaque objects are removed from the paper, the unexposed portions of the prints will also develop, especially if the paper is kept in bright daylight. To avoid this, the finished prints can be treated for five minutes in an ordinary photographic fixing bath. The images

The basic materials for the sungram project are P.O.P., fixer, and a tray.

Place the objects on the P.O.P., put the arrangement in sunlight, and wait for the paper to turn purplish-brown.

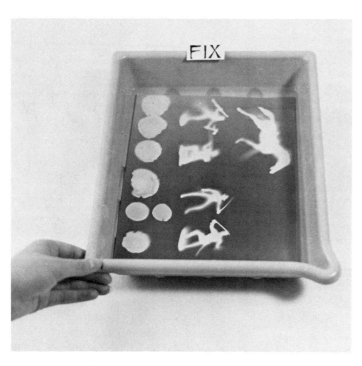

After removing the objects, place the print in the fix for about four minutes for permanence.

will then be permanent. After fixing, wash the prints in running water for about ten minutes. Drain each print completely to remove excess water and place it **face up** on clean paper toweling to dry overnight.

Fixing prints for permanency is not essential when working with very young children. The prints will last long enough for the children to get full satisfaction from the experience, providing you keep the prints away from bright sunlight after they have been completed.

If fixing the prints for more permanency is to be pursued, exposure of the paper should be two times that for a normal-density print. The image formed should appear much darker than would normally be desired. The color of the image should be a deep, chocolate brown with a slight tinge of green. Fixing these prints for the proper amount of time in a photographic fixing bath will bleach the images and cause them to lighten to the correct density.

The normal color of P.O.P. after fixing is reddish brown. If you would like to maintain the nice chocolate-brown color displayed by the paper just before fixing, dissolve three or four heaping tablespoons of ordinary table salt in the fixing bath. The resulting chocolate-brown color will be just luscious.

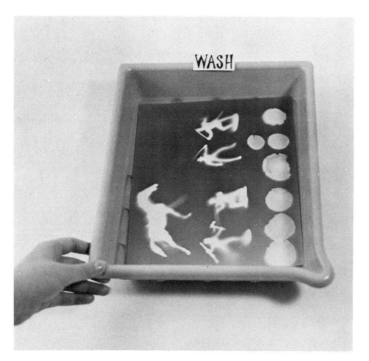

Wash the prints in a tray under running water for ten minutes, interleaving constantly.

Drain the prints and blot them with paper towels, then dry overnight, face up on clean paper.

Since the surface (emulsion) of the P.O.P. is quite fragile when wet, be very careful in handling the prints during the wet stages of the process (fixing and washing). To create a harder surface on the finished print, add some household alum to the fixer. This acts as a hardener for the P.O.P. Alum is available in most drug stores and comes in several sizes. The three-ounce size should be enough to get you started. If you intend to use alum more often in the processing, buy the 16-ounce size. It's more economical. Dissolve one to two teaspoonfuls to a pint of fixer to make a working solution.

Making images with P.O.P. can provide children with an interesting learning experience as well as a unique introduction to the photographic process. Experimenting with P.O.P. is an excellent way to acquaint children with the basic negative—positive concept of photography. It should be pointed out that the images formed by the sungram and photogram techniques are actually **negatives**, because the silhouettes produced are the result of light **not** reaching that part of the paper on which the objects are placed. Since the light does not pass through opaque objects, only the area surrounding the objects is exposed, thus creating a negative image.

A positive image can be created by placing a

Students at High Hill School in Madison, Conn., setting their finished sungrams out to dry.

Flatten the prints by placing them under several heavy books.

Here is the final result.

15

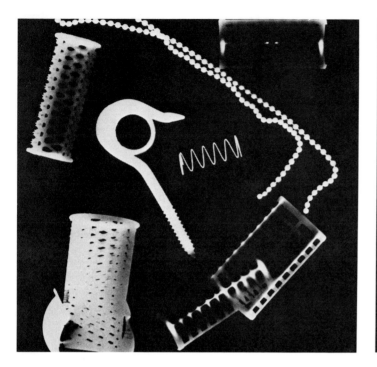

Here are some results. See how even the most common object can be used to make an interesting design.

finished sungram on another piece of P.O.P. (emulsion to emulsion), placing a piece of heavy plate glass over the two pieces of paper, and exposing the sandwich to very strong sunlight. Approximate exposure is 30 to 40 minutes, again depending on light conditions and the density of the original sungram. If the light is strong enough and the exposure long enough, another image will result which is the reverse of the first. This is the positive image.

The making of sungrams is a simple and practical way of introducing children to the print-making phase of photography. The results are immediately visible to the child as he removes the objects from the P.O.P. If in any way the print is not satisfactory, another can easily be made. Discoveries are spontaneous and natural. And it's fun!

Project 2:

More Sun Pictures

Sungrams, as described in Project 1, are an easy way to introduce children to photography without spending much money on hardware. In that project, we showed how you and your child can make pictures using printing-out paper (P.O.P.) and objects from the home. Now we will take that process one step further. Using clear, transparent Con-Tact paper and a picture from a magazine, you and your child can make an image reminiscent of sepia-toned prints.

All you need is a yard of the clear Con-Tact paper, a few sheets of Kodak Studio Proof F paper, and a tray or dish of ordinary photographic fixer. Con-Tact is available in most hardware or discount stores, and the Kodak Studio Proof F paper should be a stock item at your local photo shop. If you find that your local photography store doesn't carry this particular paper, order some. Your dealer should be able to get the paper for you in a couple of weeks.

The whole secret of this project lies in the Studio Proof F paper. It is sensitive only to ultraviolet light or direct sunlight, permitting you to use it under normal room lighting without fear of exposing it. It also develops by itself as you expose it to sunlight, eliminating the need for a developing solution. The only solution you need is a fixer to preserve the image that you create during exposure.

Now here's how to proceed. Select any image that is printed in a magazine. Most magazines are printed on a clay-base paper that facilitates the transfer of the ink on these papers to the Con-Tact. The plastic Con-Tact has a sticky adhesive substance on the side that is covered with a protective paper. Remove the protective paper and place the face of your image directly onto the sticky side of the plastic. It doesn't matter whether you place the image on the Con-Tact or vice versa, as long as you start on one side of the two pieces being bonded together and carefully work your way over to the other side. The main precaution here is to be sure not to trap air between the piece of plastic and the paper that has the printed image. Once your image and the plastic are together, burnish the image through the plastic side by rubbing it firmly with a spoon or a Popsicle stick to assure a complete cohesion between the image and the sticky part of the plastic.

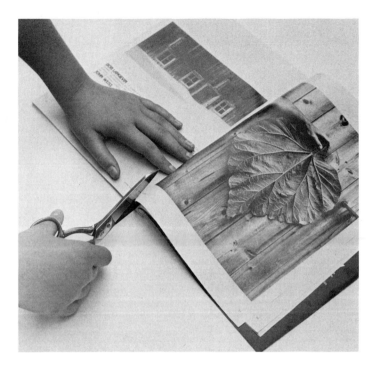

Cut out from any magazine the image that you would like to print.

Place it on a sheet of clear, transparent Con-Tact and trim to the necessary size.

17

Remove the protective backing from the Con-Tact paper.

At this point, you must soak the image and plastic in a dish of lukewarm water for several minutes. The paper base behind the image will soften enough so that you can peel it away from the image, and the image itself will remain bonded to the plastic.

After removing the paper from the image, and while the image and plastic are still in the water, gently rub the back of the image with the tips of your fingers to wash away all the milky white, clay-base residue upon which the image was originally imprinted. Blot the resulting Con-Tact image carefully between a couple of sheets of absorbent paper toweling and allow it to air-dry completely. Drying shouldn't take any longer than four or five minutes. You can hasten it by using a hair dryer on the warm-air cycle.

The dry Con-Tact image can now be used as an ordinary photographic negative. Place this image on a sheet of Studio Proof F paper (not in direct sunlight), cover the image and paper with a sheet of ordinary window glass, and place the entire sandwich in direct sunlight for exposure (a sunlamp can also be used). A printing frame can be constructed by taping a piece of window glass to a piece of cardboard or heavy mat board. Use enough tape to create a sturdy hinge.

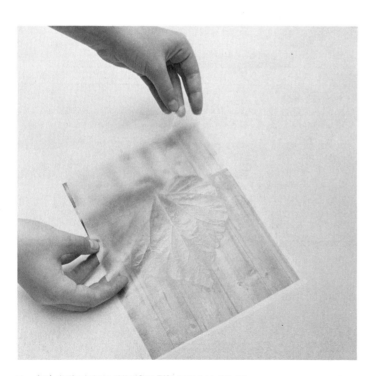

Press the sticky surface of the Con-Tact onto the printed image.

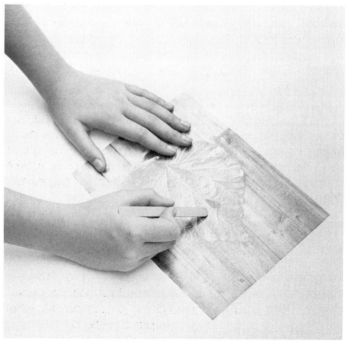

Burnish the image through the Con-Tact with a popsicle stick to ensure cohesion.

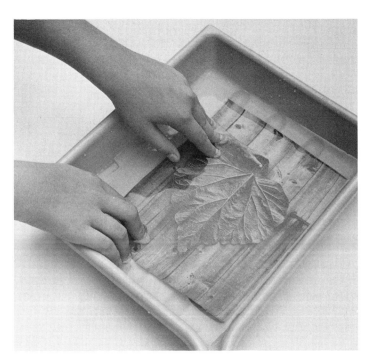

Soak the image in ordinary tap water for a few minutes.

Peel the paper from the image and rub the back with your fingertips to remove any residue.

Place the image on Studio Proof F paper, cover it with glass, and expose it to sunlight.

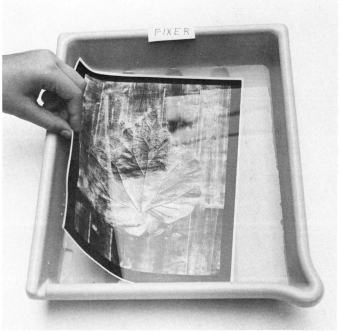

After the exposure is complete, fix the print for a few minutes for permanence.

Proper exposure of the print sandwich is simple and direct. Watch the paper under the Con-Tact image after you place it in sunlight. It soon begins to turn light purple, and within five to ten minutes, it turns from dark purple to deep chocolate brown. At this stage, exposure is complete.

Remove the print sandwich from direct sunlight, lift the glass, and separate the Con-Tact image from the photographic paper. Immediately place the exposed paper in an ordinary photographic fixing solution (mixed according to directions) and allow the print to stand in the fixer for about two or three minutes. Soon after you place the print in the fixer, it will lighten considerably. After making just a few prints, you should be able to judge very accurately just how much exposure is necessary to get the desired image density in the finished print.

After the print has been fixed for two or three minutes, wash it in a tray of cold running water for about four or five minutes. Blot the excess water from the print by placing it between two sheets of absorbent paper towel-

Wash the finished print four to five minutes in cold, running water.

Gently blot the excess water from both sides of the print with paper towels.

Pin the finished print to a bulletin board and allow it to dry for about 20 minutes.

ing. Then place it face up on another clean sheet of paper toweling to dry. Within 15 or 20 minutes, your print should be dry. When dry, the print has a tendency to curl at the edges. To flatten the print, place it under heavy books overnight.

The print that you've just made is a beautiful brownish color, reminiscent of sepia-toned prints. What you have is actually a **negative-type** print image, because the original picture from the magazine was a **positive** image. This brown-toned negative image, however, is quite exotic. The kids usually get a big kick not only out of the process, but also out of the product. The image that is produced can be mounted like any other photograph. The old-style, brown-toned quality makes it especially suitable for framing.

With a careful selection of images from magazines, you can produce a truly exotic print. Landscapes, seascapes, and architecture make intriguing subjects. Who knows, with this simple approach to making photographic prints, you may never want a camera or a darkroom!

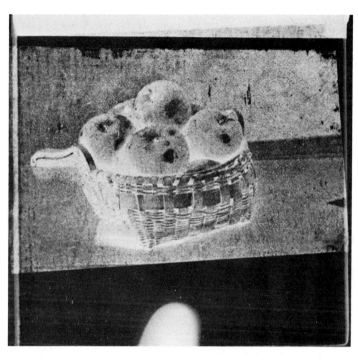

The print sandwich, when properly held, will leave a fingerprint on picture results as indicated here. To produce sharpest results, the print sandwich must be held firmly closed so that the image and P.O.P. are in perfect contact.

Note the interesting contrast in this finished print.

Students in a classroom at High Hill School, Madison, Conn., are shown printing sun pictures by sunlight with homemade print frames.

The product of the project. Remember that since the images from magazines are positive, the results will be negative.

Project 3:

Color Slides Without a Camera

Impossible? No, not really. There is a kit on the market (the Quick-Slide Kit), priced at only $4.25*, that enables you to make full-color or black-and-white slides for any 2" × 2" slide projector in only two minutes without using a camera, a darkroom, or any chemicals. As with the sun pictures described in Project 2, this system utilizes pictures cut from various magazines

Here's what you get for your money: a 2" × 2" framing device made of cardboard, a tongue depressor, a small sponge, 20 2" × 2" plastic slide mounts, and 20 pieces of plastic film. Also included is a sheet of illustrated instructions so clearly written that any child who reads can easily follow them.

The entire process takes only a few minutes. First, choose the image you want to make into a color slide. Place the 2" × 2" framing device over the image and, following the inside edges of the frame, draw a line around the image. With scissors, cut your image just outside the line that you inscribed. Next, peel the plastic film from its paper backing. (Save the backing sheet for burnishing.) Then lay the film, sticky side up, on a smooth, flat surface. Press the cutout image side down, against the sticky surface of the film. Turn over the film so that the image is visible. Using the piece of paper backing for protection, burnish the surface of the film with the tongue depressor. Then inspect the picture carefully to make certain that there are no air bubbles between the image and the film.

Soak the picture sandwich in a bowl of ordinary tap water for approximately two minutes to soften the paper the image is printed on. Next, peel away this soft, wet paper and place the film, sticky side up, on a clean, flat surface. Sponge off any white, chalky residue. You now have the image on the film.

Next, dip a plastic slide mount in water to remove surface lint. Then press the film image, sticky side down, onto this mount. Dry the image; then, with the tongue depressor, burnish the film to the mount. Trim any excess film from around edges of the mount, and there you have it,

*All prices included in this book are subject to change at the manufacturers' discretion.

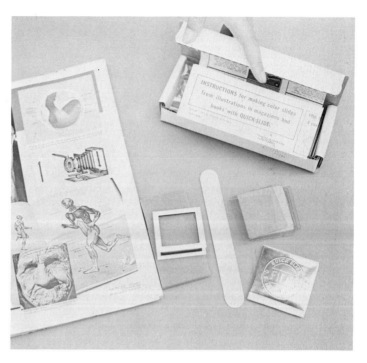

The Quick-Slide Kit includes viewfinder, film, burnishing stick, sponge, and mounts.

Place the viewfinder on the image selected and draw a pencil line around the picture.

Using scissors, cut out the image just outside the guidelines.

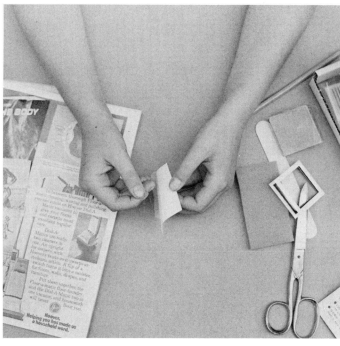

Peel the film from its paper backing. Retain the backing for burnishing.

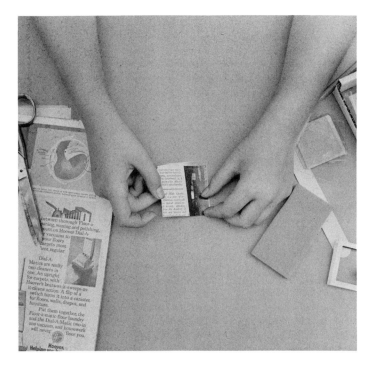

Press the printed surface of your cutout onto the sticky side of the film.

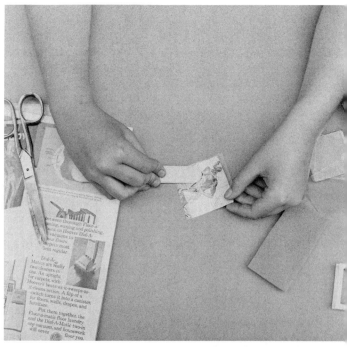

Burnish the film, image side up. For added protection, place the paper backing on the film.

fait accompli—a full-color slide that you can pop into any 2″ × 2″ projector.

Obviously, the Quick-Slide Kit, inexpensive as it is, is still too costly to be used with a large group of children. The cost of providing every child in the group with a kit would be prohibitive. Let's reexamine the materials found in the kit to see how we can find a cheaper way to present the same experience.

The kit is comprised of a viewfinder, some "film," a burnishing stick, a cellulose sponge, and plastic slide mounts. The heart and soul of the kit is the "film," which is not really film at all, but rather a material similar to clear, transparent Con-Tact, which can be purchased by the yard in most hardware and discount stores. Con-Tact is not exactly the same material, but it works just as well.

It is in the manufacture of the slide mounts that the producers of this kit have demonstrated a bit of ingenuity. These 2″ × 2″ squares of 1/16-inch Plexiglas with rounded corners **do** make very nice slide mounts. They are a little difficult to duplicate unless you are friendly with your local glazier. If he is a patient man, he can furnish you with hundreds of 2″ × 2″ plastic mounts from a single, large sheet of Plexiglas. These mounts are especially nice to use

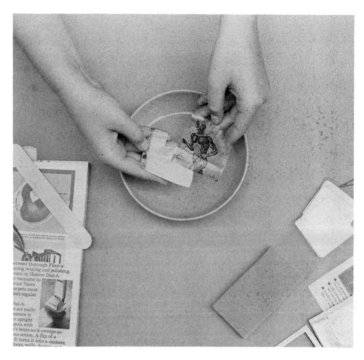

Soak the combination in water for two minutes. Then peel away the paper that the image was printed on.

Sponge away the milky residue and rinse the film well.

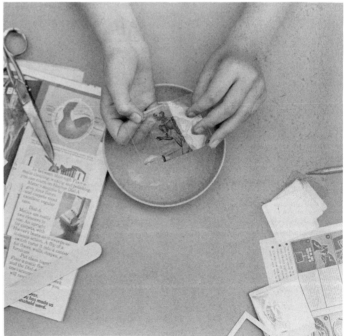

Rinse the slide mount and, centering the image, press the sticky side of the wet film onto the mount.

Dry the mounted image and trim off the excess plastic.

with very young children. If you're working with older children, you'll find that they can safely handle glass mounts, which are much cheaper than Plexiglas mounts. Most photo stores carry Kodak's 2″ × 2″ slide-cover glass mounts. A box of 50 is cheap enough to completely rationalize their use. A little plastic tape around the outside edges helps prevent chipping or scratching of the slides when you slip them into or out of the projector.

Of course, there are other types of slide mounts on the market that can be very efficiently used with children of any age, provided you don't mind the price. Snap-together plastic and glass slide mounts are sold in a variety of sizes. They come in half-frame, super-slide, 35mm, and 126, all of which will fit any 2″ × 2″ slide projector. They're convenient and reusable, but not all that cheap.

The slides made by the process featured here have their own peculiar quality, completely different from the quality of an image produced with a camera. Since pictures in a magazine have been screened to a series of black-and-white dots, your Quick-Slides will magnify this dot pattern when they are projected on a screen. Though the dot effect is pronounced, it must not be construed as a disadvantage!

Experimenting with the transfer image in slide form can provide many interesting visual effects. Seeing what happens to a small 2″ × 2″ cutout image when it is enlarged to screen size provides a touch of the spectacular. Several slide images can be combined in a slide mount to produce pictures that look like double exposures. When the sandwich is projected, it appears to be an intentional double exposure that was produced by a camera. The visual effect can be quite bizarre.

Quick-Slide Kits are available in two sizes—a 20-slide kit for $4.25 and a 75-slide kit for $14.50. They are available from Edmund Scientific Co. or Quick-Slide.

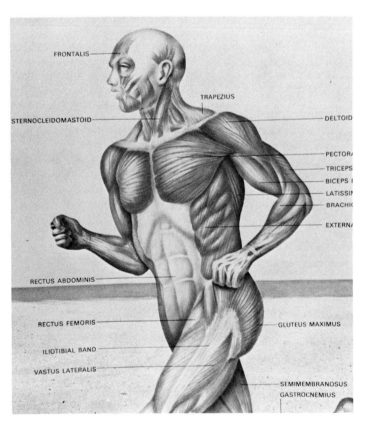

The finished slide is now ready for any 2″ × 2″ projector.

Project 4:

Pinhole Camera

Most photography buffs have made pinhole cameras before. In fact, it's really a fun way to get started in photography without spending much money. The basic materials are readily available—an old shoe box, some black paint, a piece of heavy aluminum foil, and some masking tape. By using ordinary photoenlarging paper and the proper chemicals, you can produce some very interesting results with a pinhole camera.

Instead of using a shoe box or some other square or rectangular box, try making a pinhole camera out of a ready-made oatmeal box. Since the oatmeal box is cylindrical rather than rectangular in shape, the photographic results that can be achieved are quite surprising, if not actually astonishing! Where a rectangular-type box produces a more normal-looking picture in terms of perspective, the oatmeal box, because of its curvilinear shape, delivers an outlandishly distorted image. This type of image is quite similar in many respects to the extreme wide-angle perspective changes produced by the expensive wide-angle lenses used by many professional photographers. With an oatmeal-box camera, you can simulate those wild fisheye distortions that were so prevalent a few years ago when the use of extreme-wide-angle lenses came into fashion.

The oatmeal-box camera could be a boon to the classroom teacher who would like to find an inexpensive and easy way to get started in photography. Since most households with young children use plenty of the stick-to-the-ribs cereal for breakfast, a trusty supply of oatmeal boxes to make pinhole cameras from should be easy to get. Just buy a couple of cans of nonglossy black spray paint, and you're ready to help your kids produce their own wide-angle cameras.

Any type of cylindrical box can be used to make a pinhole camera, but an oatmeal box offers a special convenience that makes it particularly well suited to this project. For example, Quaker Oats comes in two sizes—18- and 42-ounce boxes. The 42-ounce box will accept a full sheet of 8″ × 10″ enlarging paper vertically (the box is actually 9½ inches tall) with very little trimming. The 18-ounce size will take a full 5″ × 7″ sheet of paper placed the same way.

Oatmeal boxes come in two sizes: the 42-ounce size is for 8″ × 10″ pictures and the 18-ounce size is for 5″ × 7″ pictures.

Cut an opening in the side of the container for the pinhole aperture.

Spray paint the inner and outer surfaces with nonglossy black paint.

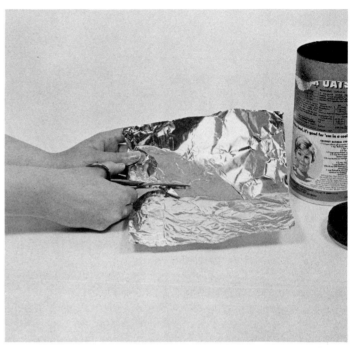

Cut a 3″ × 3″ section of aluminum foil and smooth it out on a flat surface.

Prick the foil with a straight pin, then rotate the foil to ensure the puncture.

If you're working with a group of children, it's best to use a standard box size to make the cameras. This in turn permits you to use a standard enlarging paper size for making the pictures. Therefore, the paper can be precut and ready to go at all times. It simplifies the scramble in the dark when the kids are loading their cameras. You would be surprised how much havoc a couple of odd-sized oatmeal boxes can cause at this stage.

Cut a hole in the side of the box, but make sure you use a sharp mat knife or a single-edge razor blade. Don't try to cut a round hole! You'll end up with a ragged-edged mess. Make four straight cuts to produce a nice, clean, square opening in the side of the container. Remember that the pinhole is going to be your aperture, so don't be too concerned about the opening in the side of the box. It should be about 1″ × 1″.

Next, spray paint the inside of the box—a very important step. This helps reduce unwanted reflections on the inside of the camera, which might tend to degrade image quality. You can paint the outside of the box, but this is purely cosmetic if you don't mind having that wholesome, cheery face peering out at you from the side of the red-and-blue box.

Producing the pinhole can be as simple or as complex an undertaking as you wish to make it. When

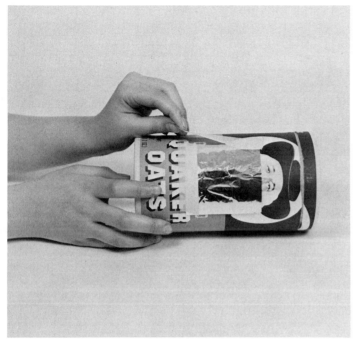

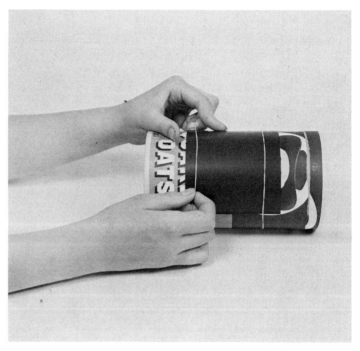

Center the pinhole over the cutout opening and secure it on all sides with masking tape.

Cut out the shutter from thin, black poster board and attach it with two rubber bands.

working with children, the simplest approach is usually preferable. Cut a 3" × 3" section of heavy aluminum foil from a roll of ordinary commercial wrapping foil. Aluminum foil is available in any supermarket. Some stores even carry the extra-heavy foil, which is even better, but the more common heavy variety is perfectly suitable.

Smooth out the cutout section on any hard, flat surface (formica, glass, or stainless steel) and use a common straight pin to prick the foil. A measure of care should be exercised when making the pinhole in the foil. Placing the foil on a hard surface helps prevent the pin from penetrating too far, which could produce too large an aperture. Gently place the pin vertically in the center of the foil section. Once the foil has been pricked, rotate the foil slightly to insure a puncture.

So there you have it—a perfect pinhole aperture, except that the hole is of an unknown diameter. But don't panic! Our procedure for determining the proper exposure is purely empirical—no math, no calculations, just a bit of commonsense trial and error. Of course, with very little experimentation, you should quickly discover for yourself that the exposure time is somewhere between 10 and 15 minutes, depending upon the brand of enlarging paper used. Place the aluminum foil with the pinhole over the outside of the cutout opening in the oatmeal box (you

Load your new camera with enlarging paper in a dark room or a dark closet.

can peek into the box to see if the pinhole is centered) and then secure it on all four sides with masking tape.

With your camera and aperture completed, all you will need now is a shutter. You can cut out what we like to call the "barn door" from a piece of thin, opaque poster board. Install it over the pinhole using two rubber bands around the box to hold it in place. Check to see that it will slide to the left or right of the pinhole without too much trouble. If it is too tight, use longer rubber bands. The sliding barn door is a simple but effective shutter mechanism.

With your pinhole camera completely assembled, all you have to do is load your camera with a sheet of ordinary enlarging paper in a dark room or a dark closet. You can now begin to make pictures—the fisheye type that seem to turn the most ordinary scenery into extraordinary images. In Project 5, we'll get into exposing, processing, and printing your pinhole extravaganzas.

A student is shown pointing the camera in the direction of a subject to determine picture content.

Here's an example of what happens to a picture when the pinhole aperture is not covered prior to picking up the camera. The sun makes a black line on the negative (bottom, left), which in turn prints as a white line on the positive print (bottom, right).

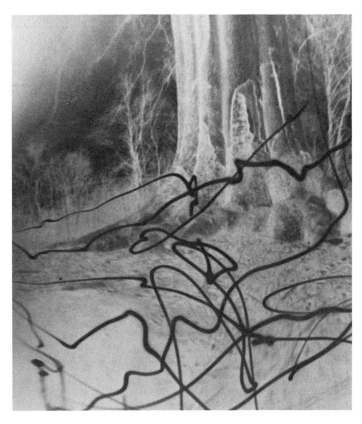

Project 5:

Pinhole Pictures

Making and using pinhole cameras with children is a marvelous way to turn kids on to photography. In the last project, we went through the step-by-step process of making a pinhole camera out of a common oatmeal box. Now we're actually going to use that pinhole camera to produce some rather exotic-looking photographs.

    Once the camera has been completed, load it in the dark with a sheet of ordinary photoenlarging paper. Since ordinary enlarging paper is not sensitive to red light, you can easily make a very practical (and portable) safelight to illuminate the situation by placing a piece of red gelatin over the front of a flashlight. If you're a teacher who doesn't have a small room in your classroom that can be totally darkened, try to get your custodian to let you use his broom closet temporarily. It can serve as a suitable temporary darkroom if you block out the light coming in from under the door with an old towel or some other material. Actually, if you're doing this project at home, any clothes closet can be quickly converted into a darkroom in the same manner.

    In Project 4, we indicated that the small oatmeal box takes a 5″ × 7″ sheet of paper, vertically, and the larger box takes an 8″ × 10″ sheet the same way, providing you trim ½ inch off the long side of the paper. Load your camera by placing a sheet of photographic paper inside the box, making sure that the emulsion side of the paper is **facing** the pinhole side of the box. The tension on the paper that is created by placing it along the curved interior of the box is just enough to hold it in place. Put the cover back on the top of the box, and you're ready to emerge into the daylight to make your first test exposure. A vertical picture can be taken by standing the camera upright with a rock on top to hold it steady. For horizontal pictures, prop the camera on its side and secure it with stones on both sides so it won't roll.

    For best results, limit all your picture-taking to bright, **sunlit** situations. A very small pinhole demands longer exposures but produces sharper pictures. A larger pinhole shortens exposure but causes more fuzzy-looking results. So a good exposure time to start with (providing your pinhole is small enough) is about ten minutes. Remember that the image must be developed in order to make it visible.

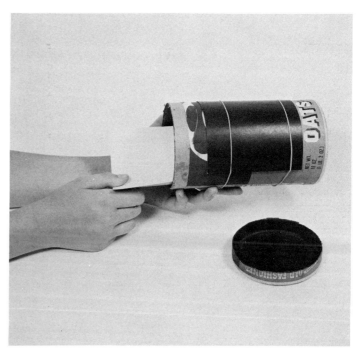

Load and unload the camera in the dark or under a red safelight. Use ordinary enlarging paper; place it vertically on the inner wall, emulsion side opposite the covered pinhole.

Take the camera out in bright daylight and take a picture.

Process the exposed paper with Dektol, Rapid Fixer, and water in darkroom trays or, in a pinch, glass baking dishes, dishpans, or square metal baking pans lined with Saran Wrap.

Use Kodak Dektol for developing and Kodak Rapid Fixer for fixing. Developing of the photoenlarging paper can proceed under red light (a red-colored flashlight will do) for two minutes with constant agitation. Drain the print thoroughly before slipping it into the fixer. (Drain time is included in developing time.) Then fix the image for four minutes in Rapid Fixer, agitating constantly. Be sure a picture is properly fixed before you look at it under normal room lighting to make certain the image is permanent. Keep the developing time constant, changing only the exposure to get the desired results. If your first picture turns out too dark or too light, adjust your exposure time up or down in five-minute increments until you can get perfect exposures every time in bright sunlight.

Each pinhole camera must be tested individually to determine the proper exposure for a given brand and grade of enlarging paper. The exposure shouldn't vary, provided that the lighting conditions and developing time remain constant. In actual practice, most of the cameras will indicate an exposure time of somewhere between 10 and 15 minutes.

When you feel that you've made all the photos you're going to make for the day, wash them in a tray under running water for 15 or 20 minutes. If you are using resin-coated papers, a four minute wash in running water

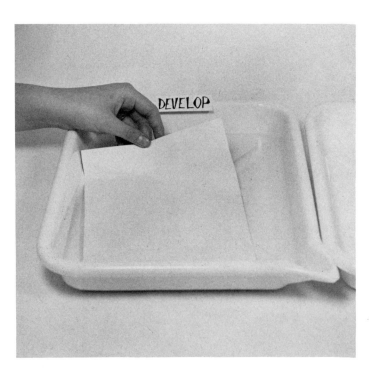

Slip the exposed paper in the developer for two minutes. Agitate it by rocking the tray gently.

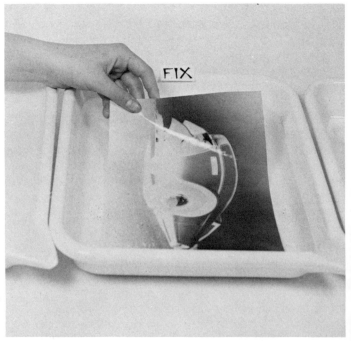

Drain the print thoroughly before slipping it into the fixer. Agitate for four minutes.

is sufficient. During the washing cycle, interleave the prints constantly to assure a more thorough washing. Then blot them between paper toweling and pin them to a bulletin board or lay them out on clean paper toweling to dry overnight. If you find that the pictures have curled after drying, place them under heavy books until they flatten out completely.

The pictures produced by the pinhole camera aren't the final prints, but rather paper negatives. These paper negatives must be contact-printed on other sheets of enlarging paper to produce positive images. To contact-print a paper negative, simply place it **over** a sheet of ordinary enlarging paper (emulsion to emulsion), cover with a clean sheet of plate glass, and expose the whole sandwich to a bright light source for a number of seconds. The exact exposure time can be determined by exposing the first print in several steps at ten-second intervals (test strip).

For example, expose the whole print sandwich for ten seconds. Next, cover a quarter of the paper at one end and expose three-quarters of it for another ten seconds. Cover another quarter and expose the remaining half for ten seconds more. Cover a third quarter and expose the last quarter for another ten seconds. When you've finished, you should have four steps at ten-second

When working in the dark or with a red safelight, place the paper negative on top of an unexposed sheet of enlarging paper, face to face. Cover the sandwich with a sheet of glass.

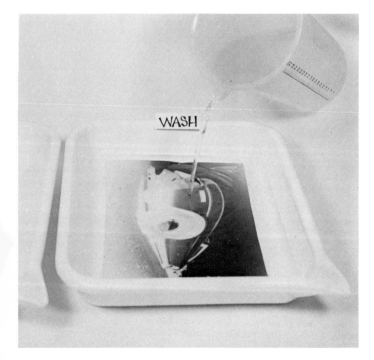

Wash the paper negative for 15 minutes in running water. (If you are washing more than one paper negative, interleave constantly.)

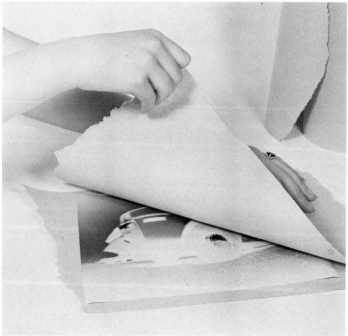

Blot the paper negative between paper toweling and allow it to dry.

increments, reading as folllows: 10, 20, 30, and 40 seconds. Remember that exposure is also affected by the brightness of the light source as well as its distance from the print sandwich.

Process the results the same way you did the paper negative. Select the best exposure from the test and make the final print for the indicated number of seconds. Keep processing times constant—developing, two minutes; fixing, four minutes. With a few trial-and-error prints, you should be able to make beautiful positive prints from your paper negatives with very little effort.

The same negative can be reprinted as many times as you wish. Bear in mind that developing and fixing **must** take place only under red light or other appropriate safe-light conditions. Photoenlarging paper is very sensitive to normal room light or daylight. Any kind of temporary dark-room setup is suitable. Even a sink isn't really necessary; just three trays and a red bulb will do.

Oatmeal-box cameras produce fascinating wide-angle photographs when the aperture, or hole, is in the **side** of the box. For some spectacular telephoto effects, try placing the aperture at one **end** of the oatmeal box. Using cylindrical oatmeal containers to produce experimental pinhole cameras can be a whole photography course in itself.

Expose the print sandwich to white light to make the final print. The best exposure can be determined with a test strip (see text). Process, wash, and dry the positive exactly as the negative: developing, two minutes; fixing, four minutes.

Look at what a pinhole camera did to the image of this automobile.

Project 6:

The Less-Than-a-Dollar Camera

How often do you hear people say, "I would like to try some photography with my kids, but cameras are just so expensive." And, you know, they're right; even the inexpensive Kodak Instamatics aren't exactly cheap. The high price of cameras is a major stumbling block that prevents many children from ever having an opportunity to experience photography first hand.

So how can you cut camera cost and still come up with a genuine photographic experience that can be shared with kids? The answer is easy enough—**use toy cameras.** This is not in any way meant to be facetious. There are some very inexpensive cameras that were never intended for the serious camera market. They were designed primarily as novelty items to be either given away as sales gimmicks or sold as toys. Yet, these toy-like cameras really work. They're a great way to introduce children to photography without spending much money on a camera.

These days it seems that nearly everyone is discovering that little gem of a camera imported from Hong Kong called the Diana. A primitive but utterly usable instrument, it is well suited to those potentially destructive little hands that just can't wait to go click click with the single-action shutter. It looks and feels very much like a 35mm camera. The entire camera is made of plastic, including the lens. It also comes with a lens cap, a neck strap, and a sheet of operating instructions. The Diana has a single shutter speed for instant exposure, and three apertures for bright, cloudy/bright, and dull weather. The camera also has three distance settings—portrait, group, and scenery.

The ease with which the camera operates is phenomenal. In any typical sunlight or bright-light situation, the camera is foolproof. To take a picture, simply set the aperture and the distance, frame the subject through the large, square viewfinder, and press the shutter. The latent image is recorded on the film, and a picture has been taken. Turn the advance knob to the next frame, and the camera is ready for another picture. Following this procedure, 16 pictures can be made on a single roll of standard 120 film.

The Diana, a cheap, fun-to-use camera, uses any standard 120 film.

Keep the camera out of direct sunlight when loading and unloading the film. Turn the catch at the base of the camera to "Open" and slide off the back cover.

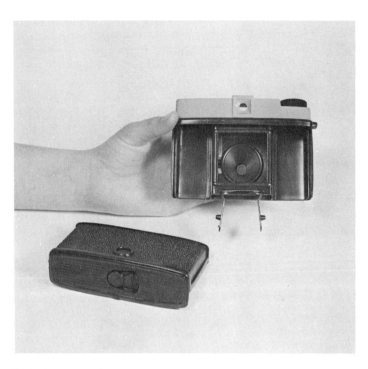

Lower the spool holders gently. Be careful with the holders because their tension mechanism can break.

In using the Diana camera, the old saying comes to mind, "It's so easy, even a child can do it." And so it is. Children seem to orient themselves to the camera even more quickly than adults, because they are not inhibited by any preconceived notions about cameras or camera operation. They just see and shoot. The camera readily becomes an "extension of the eye."

The instructions packed with the camera say nothing about the film that should be used, except that it should be 120, so any 120 film can be used. Kodak's Verichrome Pan, Plus-X, and Tri-X produce good results. In fact, the added density (darker negatives) produced by the faster type film, Tri-X, makes the resulting negatives easier to print when using a bright light source. Since any 120 film can be used in the camera, try to buy some of the inexpensive house-brand film sold by many mail-order companies or in department stores such as Sears.

With the Diana, the mechanics of film loading require a bit of care. First, you must remove the back of the camera by releasing a twist lock at the base. This allows the back portion to slide along two channels on each side of the body. Inside, place the empty spool on the right side and the spool with the film on the left. Pass the paper tongue of the film from left to right, being sure that the paper is feeding smoothly into the take-up spool before the back of the camera is closed. If the paper tongue is being crimped on either edge by the take-up spool, remove it and start again. Smooth operation of the film-transport mechanism depends on proper installation of the film.

Once the film is in the camera, turn the wind knob on the top while looking through the small red window on the back of the camera until "1" appears. Now you're ready for the first picture.

A word of caution: Remember to remove the lens cap from the front of the camera before making an exposure. By the same token, keep and use the lens cap supplied with the camera. Since the lens is plastic, any dirt that accumulates on the lens surface must be cleaned very carefully. A plastic lens is marred or scratched much more easily than one made of glass. In order to prevent the loss of the lens cap, tape a piece of string to the cap at one end and to the camera body at the other end.

It is also helpful to apply some masking tape along the back of the camera where the back slides into place. This helps minimize the possibility of light leaking into the camera, which can cause black streaks on the film. The camera manufacturer has also taken the light-leak problem into consideration. They've designed the camera to produce a 1⅝" × 1⅝" image on what is usually a 2¼" × 2¼" format field. This does help, because if a light leak

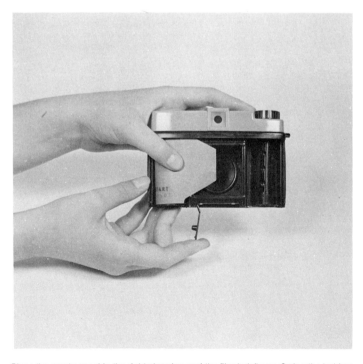

Place the empty spool in the right chamber and the film in left one. Swing the holders back in place before advancing the film.

Advance the tapered end of the film under the channel at the upper part of the camera and insert the paper tongue into the slot in the empty spool.

Turn the winding knob slowly in the direction of the arrow to ensure proper tracking, then replace the back cover and turn the catch to "Lock."

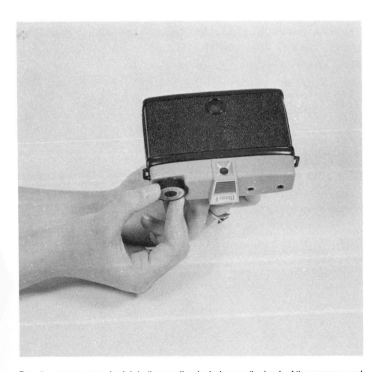

Turn the camera over, look into the small red window on the back of the camera, and advance the film until the number "1" appears in the window.

To unload the film after exposure, turn the winding knob until the film is completely wound onto the take-up spool. Open the camera and remove the film for developing.

Now with the basics out of the way, you and your child are ready to go out and shoot pictures. Upcoming projects include simple developing and processing techniques.

should occur, it usually does not enter the actual picture area. But, for the price, you can't expect the camera to perform like a professional SLR.

Now just where do you purchase a Diana? It's quite unlikely that you'll find it sitting on the shelf at your local photo dealer. There simply is no profit margin in selling $1 cameras. However, your local arts-and-crafts shop may stock it as a novelty item. It is sometimes sold under the brand name of Banner, but it's the same camera. If you can't buy the Diana locally, mail order is a must. Cameras can be ordered from Sax Arts and Crafts for $1.60 plus shipping charges. An even cheaper outlet for these cameras is the wholesale dealer, but you must order by the case (72 cameras per case). Cost is 99¢ each plus shipping charges from Power Sales Company. (See the last section of this book, "Sources and Resources," for the addresses of these companies.)

In addition, the Workshop For Learning Things, Inc. bases their whole approach to photography with kids on the Diana camera. They put out information on teaching photography to children, including inexpensive camera-and-film experiences. See their catalog for novel learning materials for teachers. They not only sell software, but all hardware (in both small and large quantities) as well.

Good luck with your Diana; it's quite a camera. And with today's prices, who knows, you might even decide to join your kid's Diana adventures and trade down to that spunky little camera yourself.

Project 7:

The Snapshooter Camera

At last a camera that little hands can handle! There's no film to load and no camera settings to become frustrated with. All you have to do is point the camera and shoot away. If this is not enough, you can also eliminate all the processing headaches that usually go along with any picture-taking project. You simply mail the exposed film cartridge off to the company and get back some big 3½″ × 3½″ pictures for your efforts.

Sounds easy? Well, it is! The Snapshooter camera is probably one of the simplest cameras ever produced. It is nothing more than a small, black box with a lens, shutter, and viewfinder that mounts directly onto the front of an ordinary Instamatic cartridge. You have to see it to believe it. The camera not only works, it actually makes good pictures.

The whole Snapshooter approach to photography is especially well suited to those of us who really want to get kids started in photography, but just can't bring ourselves, for one reason or another, to jump into the soup quite that wholeheartedly. The Snapshooter package helps us get our feet wet in photography while still keeping our fingers dry.

Maybe all this sounds too good to be true, but a company called Visual Motivations Company does offer such a package deal. They distribute the Snapshooter camera with film and processing as a complete package to an education-oriented market at a price that you can't afford to turn down. Their stated mission is to promote "better learning through photography." They have dubbed their Snapshooter package "The Photography Primer."

The idea is really very simple. Kodak had it years ago: "You press the button and we do the rest." With a Snapshooter camera, even your tiniest tyke is instantly turned into a competent photographer. With no photographic jargon to get hung up on, the kids can get right to work snapping pictures. They can start off concentrating on just what photography is all about, that is, "seeing." Since their vision is not hampered by a lot of technical stuff, they are immediately free to begin to explore the many visual possibilities of their environment. With a little

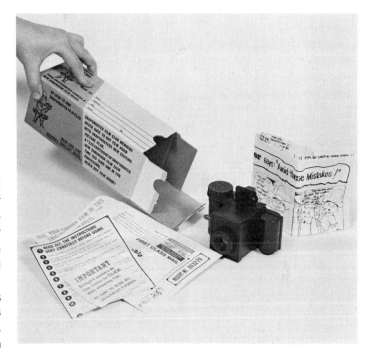

The Snapshooter package includes a camera with 126 Kodak black-and-white film (12 exposures), instructions, and a processing mailer.

The Snapshooter components, (left to right): the film cartridge, the cartridge and camera together, and the camera body only.

Wind the film slowly until a "click" sound is heard; disregard the numbers.

direction, this type of simplified approach to photography can be used by teachers and parents alike to expand and enhance practically any learning situation. It is possible for the many visual literacy fans in education to present the visual language as an integral part of almost any discipline, especially at the elementary school level.

Actually, the Snapshooter camera has been around for some time . . . as a novelty item. I've repeatedly introduced it in my workshops for classroom teachers, and to their surprise, the little "toy-like" camera produces good results. The teachers are fascinated with the tiny size of the camera and its simple mode of operation. The big plus factor often noted is that the camera itself is quite expendable. This is most important when working with young children. Cameras that are lost or broken can be readily replaced.

Occasionally, irritating light streaks showed up on some of the pictures after processing. The film cartridges, formerly manufactured in Spain, were not all that dependable. The Visual Motivations package, however, has completely eliminated this problem. Having made several modifications in the original camera, including the use of the reliable Kodak film cartridge, a new faster lens (45mm focal length at $f/8$), and a more accurate shutter that fires at a very suitable 1/125 sec., the Snapshooter

"Wow, I'm gonna take your picture!"

After 12 exposures, remove the film cartridge, starting at the opposite end from the winding mechanism and gently pry loose.

camera can now rival many of the more expensive Instamatics.

Of course, the camera has its limitations. Because it is not adjustable, you must limit all picture-taking to bright sunlit situations for the best results. It is also important to keep the camera well supported when taking pictures in order to avoid blurring the photographs by inadvertently jarring the camera. When winding the film to each subsequent exposure, you must disregard the numbers that appear in the little window on the back of the film cartridge and instead listen carefully for the audible "click" sound in the film-advance mechanism, indicating that the film has been advanced to the next frame. In short, though the camera is expendable, it must still be treated with care. Proper camera-handling attitudes should be presented to any child before he or she is given the Snapshooter to use.

A Snapshooter photo project is a practical way to get kids started in photography without the fuss and bother of setting up a darkroom. For only $2, you get the camera and a Kodak Verichrome film cartridge, a wrist strap, and a detailed step-by-step instruction sheet for handling the camera. The camera package also includes a processing mailer. Remit $1.25 plus postage with your exposed cartridge, and you'll receive, by return mail,

Neighborhood storefronts often make interesting subjects.

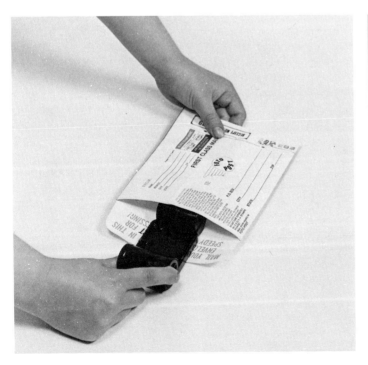
Slip the exposed cartridge into the processing mailer, enclose the fee, and mail.

The contrast between the grass and the stone gives this composition an interesting quality.

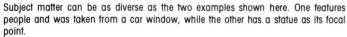
Subject matter can be as diverse as the two examples shown here. One features people and was taken from a car window, while the other has a statue as its focal point.

12 jumbo-size (3½″ × 3½″) prints. For those of you who would like to introduce kids to the actual inner workings of the Snapshooter camera, build-it-yourself camera kits are available upon request.

The Visual Motivations Company has also started to package their cameras with Kodak Tri-X film, which is especially useful for those of us who might like to process our own film. Instamatic film can be easily processed with ordinary 35mm equipment. Whether you have it processed or process it yourself, the Snapshooter camera package is a convenient way to introduce young people to a viable photographic experience.

Project 8:

Film Developing

Using inexpensive cameras and film is a good way to get children started in photography. But surely, that isn't the end of it. In fact, it's only the beginning! It isn't too difficult to teach children the mechanics of shooting pictures. Most simple cameras are very easy to load, frame, and focus, but now what?

The next step is to find a simple method to develop the film. For the method described here, you don't even need a darkroom. Kodak makes a durable plastic, daylight developing tank called Kodacraft that's easy for children to load and quite inexpensive to buy. Once the exposed film is placed into the tank, developing may proceed under any normal room lighting conditions. Of course, there's a catch. Since modern films are light sensitive, they must be loaded into the developing tank in total darkness. Use a bathroom or a closet that can be made totally dark, or a changing bag. A changing bag is nothing more than a black, lightproof cloth bag into which the hands are inserted. Buy a cheap one to see how they're constructed, and then make as many of them as you need. You may want to make a tent-like, wire structure for use inside. Since the changing bag is made of a soft fabric, the wire structure helps keep the material off your hands while loading the film into the developing tank.

The Kodacraft tank is made to accommodate various types of film simply by changing the plastic film aprons that go inside. Aprons are available for 620/120 and 127 films or for 135/126 films. The tank takes either two rolls of 135/126 film or one roll of the larger size film and holds 16 ounces of solution. It has four parts—the main body, a lightproof lid, a plastic apron with ruffled edges, and a metal weight. The lid, which snaps over the mouth of the tank, has a specially constructed hole that allows liquids to be poured in and out without exposing the film inside to light. To make sure that the lid does not drop off when pouring out solutions, hold it securely to the tank. There may be some spillage at the point where the lid fits on the tank, but this does not affect processing. However, it can be a little messy, so work on paper toweling, in a plastic dishpan, or right in the sink itself.

The best way to understand how the film you are using is put together is to sacrifice a roll and take it apart

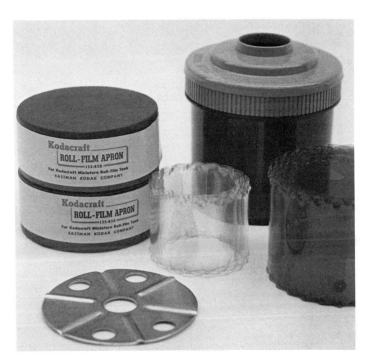

Use a roll-film developing tank with aprons available for 135/126 films and 620/120 films.

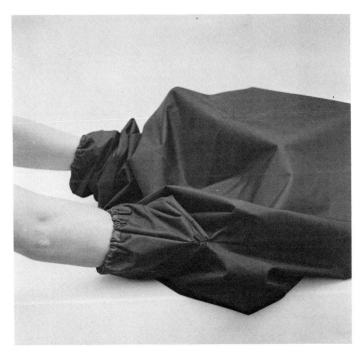

A good alternative for those without a darkroom is a lighttight changing bag.

43

Unroll the film, separate it from the paper backing, and cut the tape where they are attached.

Place the outside curl of the film into the inside curl of the apron and roll together carefully.

in broad daylight. Since you're probably using the Diana camera recommended in Project 6, the film you'll be developing is 120 roll film. This particular type of film is wrapped in paper around a plastic or metal core.

Let's assume you're using a changing bag for loading. The procedure is exactly the same as when loading a tank in the darkroom. Everything you need, including the various parts of the tank and the film, should be in the changing bag before you begin to load. First, unroll the film and separate it from its paper backing. Gently peel the film from the end where it is attached to the paper backing with tape, or cut it free with scissors. Try to handle the film by the edges while you're winding it into the plastic apron. Place the outside curl of the film into the inside curl of the apron. Roll the apron and film together and place them into the developing tank. Cover the apron and film with the metal weight and secure the lid on the tank. When rolling the film into the apron, be careful not to wind the apron too tightly around the film. The apron must be tight enough to fit into the tank, yet loose enough to permit the proper flow of solutions over the surface of the film. Once the tank is covered, film developing may proceed under normal lighting conditions.

If you're loading 126 Instamatic film into the Kodacraft tank, all of the above procedures are the same, except the opening of the cartridge itself. The 126 cartridge, like the one used with the Snapshooter camera, can be broken open by hand or with pliers, if necessary. The large end of the cartridge contains the film. Inside the 126 cartridge, you'll find that the film has a paper backing just like the 120 film used for the Diana. Separate the paper backing from the film, load the film into the 135 Kodak apron, and place it in the Kodacraft tank. Remember that the tank can accommodate two 135 aprons, one atop the other in the same tank. So you can actually develop two rolls of 126 film at a time.

The chemicals needed for black-and-white developing are few, just a developer and a fixer. The most readily available products for processing film are made by Kodak. Most photo shops and discount stores carry Kodak products. Start with D-76 film developer, which is sold in quart, half-gallon, and gallon sizes. Buy the gallon size; it's the most economical and practical quantity to use with a group of children. The D-76 developer comes in powdered form and is mixed with hot water to make a working solution. Just follow the mixing directions on the back of the can.

There are two basic types of fixer available— regular fixer and rapid fixer. Use a rapid fixer, because it cuts the usual fixing time in half and contains a film hardener which helps prevent film damage. Kodak's Rapid Fixer is packaged in two easy-to-mix concentrated solutions—fixer and hardener. To make the appropriate working solutions, these concentrated solutions are combined with water at about 70 F according to the directions on the bottle.

When mixing solutions, be sure to use containers made of plastic, glass, or stainless steel. Some great plastic pails are available for free or at a nominal cost from your local doughnut shop. Their jellies are packaged in high-quality plastic pails that are practically indestructible. Use a long plastic rod or a large plastic mixing spoon to stir your solutions. Stock solutions should be kept in dark-colored bottles. Your druggist might supply you with all the empty gallon bottles you need for free—just ask. You'll also need a measuring beaker and a funnel to prepare your fresh solutions. Keep your stock of solutions at room temperature until you are ready to use them.

The developer is the most critical solution used in film processing. Proper film developing is based on a time/temperature scale, which is printed on the small data sheet packaged with each roll of film. A timer and a thermometer are helpful accessories for film developing, but they are not absolutely necessary. Just remember that the negative becomes darker with longer developing or with an **increase** in the temperature of the developer or both. With a **decrease** in temperature and/or a shorter developing time, the negative becomes lighter. For example, the recommended time and temperature for Kodak Plus-X film is 5½ minutes in D-76 at 70 F. Since 70 F is just about room temperature, it should be fairly easy to maintain a constant processing temperature. It may be necessary to double or triple the normal development time to produce printable negatives.

Don't be afraid to overdevelop a little; the darker results may prove helpful later. Be sure, however, to gently shake the tank at regular intervals (about every 30 seconds) when you're developing. This assures even developing of the film. (If you keep the temperature of the solutions fairly constant, you can vary developing time to increase or decrease the darkness of the negative.)

After you've developed the film, pour out the developer and fill the tank with water (about 70 F) to rinse off any remaining solution. Then pour rapid fixer into the tank and shake it gently for approximately four minutes. Pour out the fixer and wash the film in the tank under about 70 F water for three or four minutes. Dump the tank periodically to insure proper washing. After the fixing, you may remove the lid and weight from the tank, because the film is no longer sensitive to light. Removing the lid and weight also

Place the film in the tank and cover it with a metal weight to keep them both in place.

Tip the tank slightly when filling it with solution to make pouring easier.

facilitates the final washing of the negative. When you are finished washing, hang up the film to dry on a line with ordinary snap-on clothespins. Be sure to place some sort of weight on the opposite end of each roll you dry. This helps minimize curling during the drying process. Do not handle any of the negatives until they are thoroughly dry.

Granted, the approach outlined here is quite rudimentary, but it does bring adequate results. When working with a group of children, it is best to simplify processing as much as possible. The method outlined here is meant to produce satisfactory results with a minimum of effort.

Hold the cover to prevent its dropping off while you empty the tank (left).

Use bulldog clamps or clothespins when hanging the film up to dry (bottom, left).

Project 9:

Photo Printing

Film developing is a relatively simple process, as you learned in Project 8. Very little practice is necessary to master the procedures involved, and once the film is developed, the latent or "hidden" images that were created in the camera are completely visible. All the images that appear on the film, however, are **negative.** This means that the tones of the original scene are reversed. What was light in the scene is dark on the film, and what was dark in the scene is almost clear on the film. The whole roll of film is nothing but a series of such negative images attached end to end. The tones in each of these negative images must be reversed in order to reproduce what was seen through the camera's viewfinder at the time of exposure.

To turn a negative image into a positive image quickly, every photographer follows a basic photographic procedure called **contact printing.** First, the negative is placed directly in contact with a piece of photographic paper. Then this negative and paper sandwich is exposed to a light source. The photographic paper must be removed from the sandwich and properly processed to produce the final positive image, which is actually a small black-and-white replica of the original scene.

Making contact prints is a very practical way to teach kids the basics of photographic printing. The primary limitation of contact printing is that it always produces an image exactly the same size as the negative. (This could actually be considered an advantage for the teacher who is dealing with a group of children in a classroom situation.) The principal advantage of making contact prints, on the other hand, is that it does not require the use of an enlarger.

In order to make contact prints the way most photographers do, some sort of "darkroom" situation is essential. At this point, many people who do not have access to the proper darkroom facilities may well ask, "How can we provide children with some sort of do-it-yourself photographic experience without using a darkroom?" The answer is simple—use P.O.P.!

Making prints with Kodak Studio Proof F P.O.P. offers the same type of experience as when using normal photographic paper, but it eliminates the need for a dark-

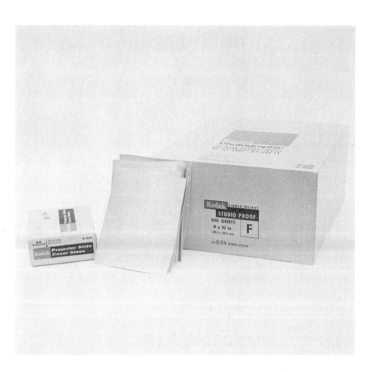

For printing without a darkroom, you can use Kodak Studio Proof F paper.

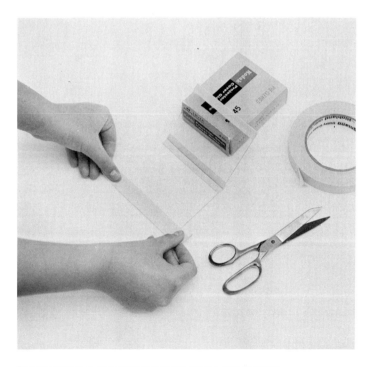

Tape two pieces of cover glass together to make a print sandwich.

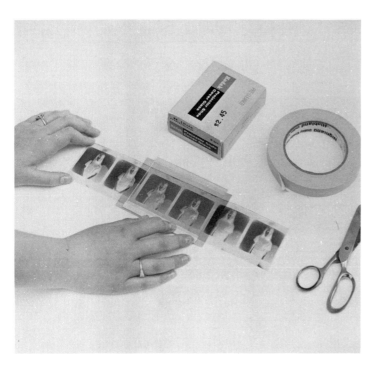

Place the negatives and paper into the sandwich for contact printing.

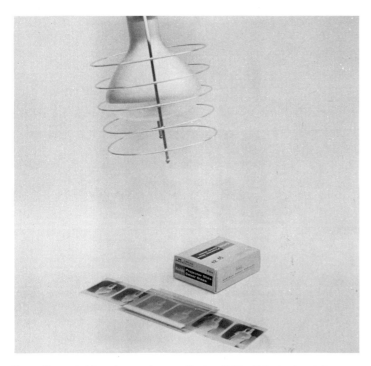

Expose the sandwich under a sunlamp or direct sunlight until the borders darken.

room. We introduced P.O.P. in Projects 1 and 2. If you recall, this paper has definite advantages. It can be handled under normal room light and requires no developer. Hence, the need for a darkroom is eliminated and chemicals are unnecessary. Any room, small or large, can instantly become a photographic workshop.

Before printing your negatives on P.O.P., you must devise some method to hold the negatives and paper in direct contact. Photographers generally use a printing frame, which is a gadget designed to hold both negatives and paper securely against a piece of glass for proper exposure to light. If your negatives and paper do not make proper contact, the images will be out of focus.

Since you're going to print only two frames from your roll of film at a time, the device used for keeping the negatives and paper in contact need not be elaborate. A very suitable printing apparatus can be made from two pieces of slide cover glass and some masking tape. Kodak sells 3¼" × 4" Projector Slide Cover Glass in boxes of 24 sheets each. Two such pieces of glass hinged on one side with tape can provide you with an excellent substitute for the printing frame. Your local glazier can also cut pieces of the size you need from some scrap glass lying around the shop; ask for a price.

You may want to tape the four sides of both pieces of glass to help prevent cuts on little hands. Of course, if you prefer not to use glass at all with little children, the same device can just as easily be created out of Plexiglas. Your local glazier should be able to supply you with the number of precut pieces you need. In either case, use a piece of masking tape to hold the print sandwich closed while printing. This assures proper contact between your negatives and paper during exposure.

Now for the printing procedure, step by step.

1. Cut your roll of negatives in strips of four or more frames each. Cutting single frames is not recommended, because this makes the negatives more difficult to handle.

2. Place the frames you intend to print on top of a piece of P.O.P. emulsion to emulsion (the emulsion side of the negative is the dull side and the emulsion side of the paper is the shiny side), put this inside the printing frame, and tape the print sandwich closed.

3. Expose the print sandwich to direct sunlight or a sunlamp, making sure that the film side of the sandwich is facing the source of light.

4. Determine exposure by watching the borders around the negatives. When the borders are very dark, exposure is complete.

Optional Steps:

5. Remove the exposed paper from the print sand-

wich and immerse it immediately in rapid fixer for four minutes.

6. Transfer the paper print to a tray of clean, fresh water, where it should stay until all printing is finished.

7. When the desired number of prints are completed, wash all finished paper prints in a tray of running water for about ten minutes. (Water and fixer should be at room temperature.) Be sure to interleave the prints during the washing cycle by continually removing the bottom print and placing it on top of the whole batch. It is also wise to dump the tray of water and refill it several times during the washing operation. Since fixer is heavier than water, it tends to settle to the bottom of the tray. Continuous interleaving of the prints and periodic dumping of the wash tray helps to promote better washing.

8. Remove the prints one by one from the wash tray, sponge off their excess water with absorbent paper toweling, and pin them up to dry. If a pinup surface is not available, prints may dry face up on paper toweling.

Fixing prints for permanence is not necessary when working with young children. Images produced with P.O.P. provide a fascinating and exciting experience for them. They can actually observe the changes that take place during and after exposure.

The purplish-brown images that result do eventually fade away, but they will last long enough for the children to get full satisfaction from the experience. In fact, seeing the images fade can also be an aspect of the learning experience. After the paper is removed from the print sandwich, the unexposed portions of the prints begin to develop and turn brown, especially if the paper is kept in bright sunlight. This effect can be minimized by keeping exposed prints away from bright lights.

If fixing prints for permanency is to be pursued, exposure should be increased considerably. Allow exposure to continue until the images formed appear much darker than would normally be desired. Fixing the prints in rapid fixer for the proper time tends to bleach the images and causes them to lighten to the correct density. By trial and error, you should be able to determine quickly just how much overexposure is necessary to produce a normal-looking print quality.

Experimenting with P.O.P. is an excellent way to acquaint children with the basic negative—positive concept of photography; it also provides a simple and practical way to introduce children to print-making. The results are immediately visible to the children as they remove the exposed paper from the print sandwich. If any of the children don't like their prints, they can easily make others. Discoveries are spontaneous and natural.

For permanence, immerse the prints in Rapid Fixer for four minutes.

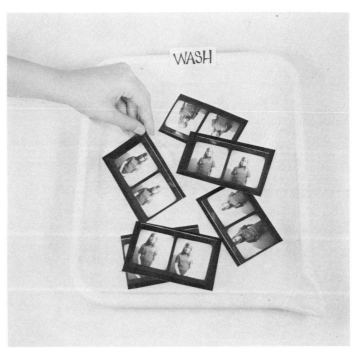

Wash the prints in a tray under running water for ten minutes, interleaving constantly.

Remove the prints from the tray and sponge off any excess water with paper towels.

Dry prints face up on a clean sheet of white paper or pin them to a wall.

Here's one of the finished products.

Project 10:

Temporary Darkrooms

You don't need a darkroom to teach kids photography. You don't even need a sink that has hot and cold running water. This was amply demonstrated in many of the projects that have already been outlined. However, if you can set up some kind of temporary darkroom situation, most do-it-yourself projects can be greatly facilitated. In addition, with a temporary darkroom, the student of photography can explore a whole range of photographic experiences that are simply impossible without it.

Setting up a temporary darkroom can be as simple or as complex as you wish to make it. There's one famous contemporary photographer who produces exquisite prints on his kitchen table in the evening with the window shades pulled down, and another who must remove the contents from a small closet in her apartment before beginning a printing session. There's just no end to the different kinds of compromise that can blossom forth when conditions are somewhat less than ideal.

Let's start off with the portable darkroom idea. As you probably already know, there are many fine daylight-type film-processing tanks available today that are designed to be used in any type of lighting. Loading these tanks, however, does require the proper darkroom conditions. You can duplicate these same conditions on a small scale by using a changing bag.

Changing bags can be purchased very reasonably at your local photo dealer. A 17" × 17" bag should cost around $6 or $7. (Considering today's inflation and price fluctuations, the cost of photographic items outlined here may differ around the country, so check with your local dealer.) The larger pro-type bag (27" × 30") offers a more convenient working space, but is about double the price. Nevertheless, it is worth buying the larger bag. All you'll need is a couple of them for any classroom situation, because the bag is used only for "loading," and can be shared.

One step up from the changing bag is to utilize a closet or any small storage room that you can periodically appropriate. Some closets have a sink, but most do not. A janitor's closet, for example, generally sports some type of all-purpose sink. Nevertheless, let's presume a closet without a sink as the base of operations. Your first task is to make the situation lightproof.

Film processing can be done in any room when a daylight tank is used.

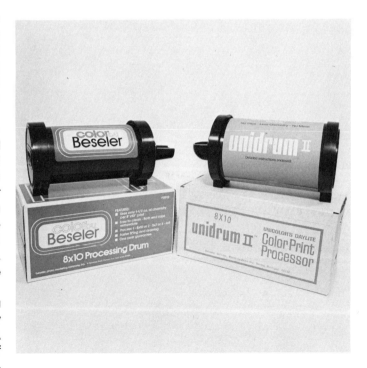

Daylight print processing also can be done with a variety of print drums.

51

A lap board is being used to load one of the reels for a daylight film tank.

Making a closet dark is not too difficult. Just sit inside the closet for a few minutes with the lights off. As your eyes begin to adjust to the darkness, any light seeping into the closet from the outside is quite apparent. The typical closet is well sealed along the top and the sides of the door. The place where light is apt to enter is under the bottom of the door. This can easily be corrected by placing a small rug, a heavy bath towel, or an old blanket along the floor on the inside of the door.

The closet darkroom can be used to load daylight film tanks prior to processing. To facilitate loading these units, use a lap board as a working surface while sitting on a chair. Processing can be carried out in the kitchen sink or in any other sink that is convenient. If there isn't a sink handy, any tabletop or counter surface will do. Spillage can be controlled during processing by spreading out a few sheets of old newspaper or absorbent paper toweling to cover the work area. A simple catch-all tray can be made by cutting a corrugated box about two inches from the bottom and lining it with thin plastic wrap, the kind garments are covered with after dry cleaning.

To produce prints in your closet darkroom, you'll need to purchase a suitable enlarger. Since closet darkrooms are usually quite small, choosing the right enlarger is most important. Rapid assembly, ease of performance, and practical storage are the most important characteristics to look for. With very little shopping, you'll soon discover that there are several relatively inexpensive enlargers for 35mm film on the market that are perfect for the temporary darkroom. The Durst F-30, for example, meets all of the aforementioned requirements and retails, without lens, for under $60. Add an inexpensive lens for about $15, and you've got a nice little package.

For school teachers, the janitor's closet is your best bet, because you have a dark room with a sink for washing the prints (top, left). Make sure you block any light leaks.

A teacher's storage closet can be emptied temporarily to serve as a darkroom. A folding table was installed here to hold the enlarger and trays (top, right).

A bathtub setup is especially practical when kids cannot reach the sink. Remember to line the bathtub with plastic to avoid staining the porcelain with solutions (right).

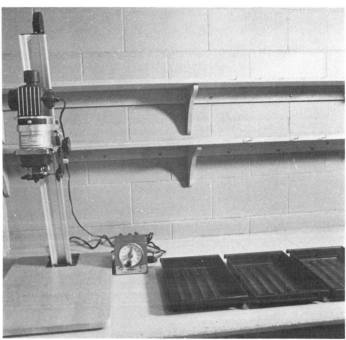

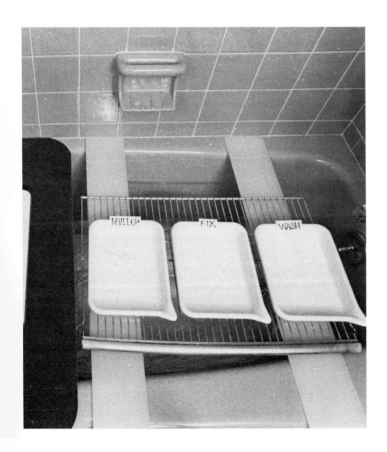

When working on a kitchen table, you can make a spillage tray from a cardboard box lined with plastic.

If your closet has a light in it, then you have all the electricity you'll need to power your enlarger. If not, just run a heavy-duty extension cord under the door to serve the same purpose. As indicated in Project 5, an ordinary flashlight with some red gelatin over it makes a cheap and practical safelight. The Bright Star Darkroom Lite is a more permanent version of the same idea. It uses two D-size batteries and has three interchangeable safelight filters—red, orange, and green. Check with your local photo dealer. He should be able to order it for you if he doesn't already have it in stock.

Now all you need is some photographic printing paper, and you're ready to make some fine enlargements. Be sure to buy the new resin-coated paper. It will save you a lot of time in the washing and drying operations. Kodabrome RC, Ilfospeed, and Unicolor all sell for about $6 to $7 per 25-sheet package of 8″ × 10″ paper.

A mechanical enlarging timer is a useful accessory for timing your print exposures, but it is not indispensable. (One summer, I had a student who produced some beautiful prints in her home darkroom, to my complete dismay, by simply counting 1,001, 1,002, and so forth.) Most enlarging timers aren't cheap, costing from about $40 to $50. You might consider Mark Time's inexpensive Photographic Time Switch ($11.50).

Once you've exposed your print, you must process it in the proper solutions. If your closet darkroom is large enough to incorporate a couple of trays full of chemicals, you can print and process your enlargements right in the same situation. If not, load your exposed enlarging paper into a daylight print drum and process it in your kitchen sink or on the kitchen table. The print drum provides a practical way of separating the dry and wet stages of the print-making, especially when space is at a premium.

As a result of the current push by the industry to popularize color printing, a number of excellent daylight print-processing drums have surfaced. Beseler, Unicolor, and Omega each put out their own drums. The convenient 8″ × 10″ size is moderately priced at about $16 or $17. They are designed primarily for color print processing, but may be used just as effectively to process black-and-white print materials. All you need to do is expose your print in the closet darkroom, slip it into the print drum, and then take the drum to the kitchen sink for the processing stage. Once the exposed paper is in the drum, processing may proceed under any normal room lighting.

Prewet the paper by filling the drum with about eight ounces of water (around 70 F for water and chemicals). Agitate by rolling the drum back and forth horizontally on a flat surface for one minute. Empty the drum and put in two ounces of paper developer (Dektol 1:2). Agitate for one minute as recommended for resin-coated papers. After developing, empty the drum and rinse it with water. Then add two ounces of rapid fixer and agitate for two minutes. After fixing, empty and wash the print in water for four minutes. Remove the print from the drum and blot it dry between paper towels.

Separating the dry and wet stages of the print-making process can be more feasibly accomplished in the same space when you're using a bathroom as a dark-room, and the running water is always an asset. Today, some houses and apartments have more than one bathroom. Turning one of them into a temporary darkroom should not cause too much inconvenience. Other homes even have a central bathroom in the floor plan, which utilizes an exhaust fan as a substitute for a window. This type of bathroom is ideally suited for the temporary darkroom, because it is as easy to lightproof as a closet. If you're using a bathroom with a window, you can light-proof the window by covering it with a heavy, opaque cloth. Tack the edges of the cloth securely to the sides of the window frame to prevent any light leak. Then all you have to do is use the closet technique for the bottom of the bathroom door.

Place your enlarger on the counter next to the sink, or cover the sink itself with a piece of heavy Masonite and use it as the counter top. Your trays of solutions can be set directly into the bathtub, or you can build a wooden rack over the bathtub to house the trays. Line the inside of the tub with a plastic drop cloth or newspapers to prevent any spotting or staining of the porcelain by the photo solutions. Mark Fineman's book **The Home Darkroom** (Amphoto, 1975, $3.95) provides some good tips on how to turn your bathroom into a darkroom. (A resources listing that outlines many sources of information related to the teaching of photography to kids is included in this book.)

Picture-taking is only half the fun of photography for kids. Getting them into the "darkroom" to develop and print their own pictures brings the mystery and magic of photography right to their fingertips. Darkroom work, even if only in a temporary situation, can do wonders to help children develop a sense of adequacy, self-control, and direction that must inevitably spill over into other aspects of their lives. Do-it-yourself picture-making need not be just a fun activity for kids; photography can actually serve as a bridge to some of our highest educational goals.

When processing the prints, plastic tops from hairspray cans provide good containers for the developer and fixer (two ounces each for an 8" × 10" drum). The jar is used for the prewet and the water is used for the rinse. The setup is over the kitchen sink.

This is the "before" scene in a basement room of an elementary school. The storage room was turned into a darkroom.

The "after" scene is shown here. The same basement room was cleared, cleaned, and painted to make an ideal darkroom situation.

Project 11:

Cartridge-Loading Cameras

Want to buy good cameras for kids at rock-bottom prices? Well, watch for the sale ads in your local newspaper. Surprisingly enough, some top brand-name cameras (as well as some less well-known brands) often sell for ridiculously low prices. Once you know exactly what kind of camera you want, you may be able to purchase it for little more than the wholesale price.

There are two basic lines of inexpensive cameras on the market—the regular 126 cartridge-loading cameras and the more recent pocket 110's. Even though there are more expensive types sold, the basic, bottom-of-the-line cartridge-loading cameras (whatever the brand name) are excellent and perfectly suitable for any kid's picture-taking needs.

The regular cartridge cameras use 126-size film, while the pocket cameras use 110-size film. The film cartridge itself incorporates both its feed and take-up spools in a single unit that slips easily into the back of the camera, thus eliminating any possible film-loading problems. This is especially helpful when working with youngsters. These cameras are no substitute for the more expensive, sophisticated cameras, but they do provide an inexpensive way to introduce children to the wonders of photography.

The 126-type camera is a good beginner's camera. Even the basic model offers an array of features. Easy loading is its most attractive characteristic. You can also load the camera in any light. Each frame is positioned and counted as you advance the film. It automatically stops at the proper position for each exposure, with frame numbers visible in the film window. There's a double-exposure-prevention shutter release that works only when the unexposed film frame is in the correct position. A bright, projected frame in the viewfinder provides picture-framing ease and accuracy. Flash can be used without batteries. A Magicube flash rotates automatically as the film is advanced, and four flash pictures can be taken without changing cubes. In many models, the viewfinder indicates the presence of either a fresh or used lamp. New FlipFlash units are available for the latest models.

Many cartridge-loading cameras are sold today. Here are two that use 126 film.

Cartridge-loading cameras are cheap and easy to use. Here are some of the 110 type.

The film cartridge is just slipped into the camera back and you're ready to shoot.

A daylight film developing tank is convenient for do-it-yourself processing of both 126 and 110 film.

All these features can be found on the more recent 110 pocket cameras. Since they utilize a smaller film size, the 110 cameras are much more compact than their 126-size cousins. Although the 110 negatives and slides are much smaller than those from 126 film, the size of the prints that can be made should be acceptable to most people. The big advantage of the pocket camera is its complete portability. Because of its size, you can literally slip it into your shirt pocket or any other small space. It's always there, waiting to be used.

These bottom-of-the-line cameras are a pleasure to use, because they can get us back to those good old box-Brownie days. With the current trend toward more and more complicated camera equipment, it's just plain fun to use a camera that doesn't require an advanced photography course before you are able to take pictures. Photography with the inexpensive cartridge-loading cameras is as uncomplicated as can be. These fixed-focus and fixed-exposure cameras free the beginner to concentrate fully on seeing and taking pictures. They provide for a degree of instant success that helps foster the confidence and courage necessary to explore the pleasures of photography.

Fixed settings on a camera can produce good pictures, providing you remember to work within the particular limits prescribed by those settings. First, fixed focus means that the camera has been factory focused to take pictures only within a specific distance range. For example, if your camera manual states that the lens is prefocused to cover a range from five feet to infinity, this means you cannot take any pictures less than five feet from your subject without appreciable blurring. So you would always have to be sure that you were at least five feet from your subject in order to keep your pictures in focus.

Second, fixed exposure means that the lens-aperture and shutter-speed combination on your camera is preset for a given exposure, which is usually bright daylight. If you attempt to take pictures in shade or indoors without flash, they will be underexposed. On the other hand, if you shoot a bright beach scene or snow scene, your negatives will probably suffer from overexposure. Negative film has a higher tolerance for overexposure than for underexposure, so you can probably get away with using your cartridge camera at the beach and achieve acceptable results.

Nevertheless, fixed-exposure cameras are a snap to use, because in most cases you are either shooting pictures outdoors in bright daylight or indoors with the proper flash. All cameras with fixed settings are designed to cover both situations with ease. Remember when you are using a flash indoors to stay within the distance limitations of your flash. You can check your camera manual for the exact limit, but it's usually somewhere between five and ten feet from your subject.

As you can see, those inexpensive cameras are a bargain in more ways than one. You not only save a lot of money on the initial purchase, but you also save yourself much aggravation later on. The film processing is also easy. (See Project 8 and Project 9 for more details.)

Today, photography with such inexpensive, simple cameras is helping to explode the terrible classroom myth that "learning can't be fun." With five or six cameras and the help of your local processor (or your own bathroom lab for that matter), you and your students can make almost any subject come alive. Since today's world is just brimming with visual learning challenges, how can we possibly rationalize an educational system that restricts practically all learning to paper and pencil? The answer is obvious—we can't. Therefore, get your P.T.A. or some local group to sponsor your adventure into photography . . . now! It's more than fun—**it's a whole new way of learning.**

The Kodak Kodacraft Roll Film Tank with 35mm apron can be used to develop 126 film.

Your child can easily take pictures without a technical photo background.

Both the 126 and 110 cameras come with flashcube-type capabilities. Here the Kodak 110 sports a new type of multiflash unit.

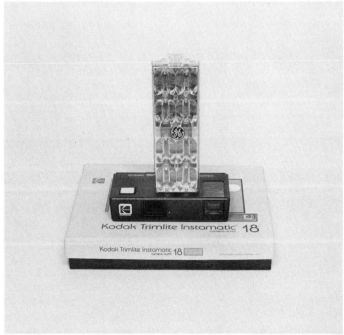

Kids, cameras, and the outdoors—a winning combination, as you can see from the photos on this and the next two pages. They were taken with 110 and 126 cartridge-loading cameras, and the subject matter was as varied as a child's imagination.

Project 12:

Photoenlarging

Contact printing negatives on photographic paper is the simplest and quickest way to produce positive images. You can immediately see what your negatives can deliver. Most children will accept contact prints as the products of their picture-taking efforts.

Contact printing, however, can only produce **negative-size** positive images of the pictures taken with any camera. So the bigger the camera, the larger the final image will be. That's why pinhole cameras can easily be made to produce decent-size images, while roll-film cameras, of necessity, depend upon an enlargement process to produce satisfying results.

Making enlargements with kids can be fun, providing you have access to a darkroom with an enlarger. Temporary darkroom situations for enlarging are easy enough to set up, as long as the cost of the hardware is reasonable.

A company called C V Products, Inc. has come up with an interesting photoenlarging kit that can help you get a darkroom started at a modest price. For only $31.95, you can purchase the C V Developing and Enlarging Kit (No. 1111), which will provide you with everything you need to develop and enlarge your black-and-white photos up to 3½" × 5".

The 18-piece kit contains the following: a UL and C.S.A. approved enlarger, an amber safelight, 25 sheets of 3½" × 5" glossy enlarging paper, two chemistry packs, a developing tank, three darkroom trays, two film clips, a graduate, a thermometer, three negative carriers, a reversible easel mask, and a step-by-step instruction booklet. The enlarger handles negative sizes for 35mm, 126, and 127 film. (The Diana's 120 film can be cut to fit the 127 negative holder, since the actual picture area is almost that size anyway.)

The enlarging process is pretty much the same whether you use the C V enlarger or not. In black-and-white photography, it's always preferable to have negatives that are slightly overexposed rather than underexposed. For example, when using Diana or Snapshooter cameras with kids, help them to see that slightly dense negatives will produce better results than thin negatives. Adequate density is a must for producing decent enlargements.

Here's what you get in an enlarging kit. (This one's from C V Products, Inc.)

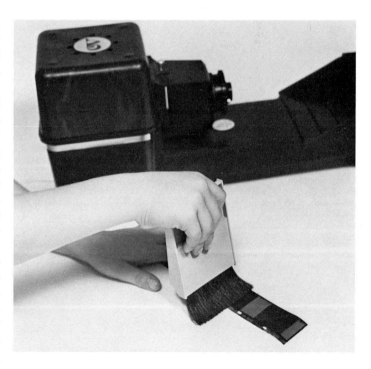

Thoroughly clean the negative to be enlarged, and then insert it in the proper negative carrier and place it in the enlarger.

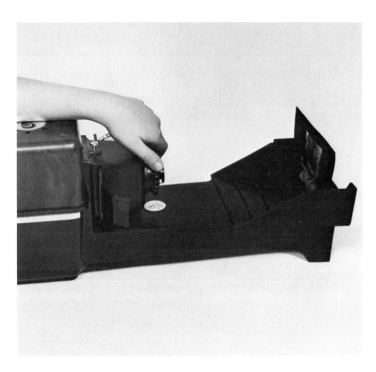

Compose and focus the picture on an easel using white paper to focus on.

Insert the enlarging paper in an easel ready for exposure.

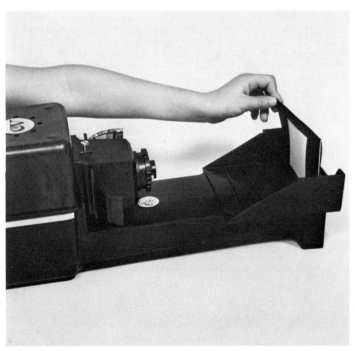

Now let's get started. First, thoroughly clean the negative to be enlarged. If you start your printing session with clean, well-exposed negatives, you should be able to produce trouble-free enlargements. Using clean negatives is really half the battle when making quality enlargements. The importance of cleanliness cannot be overemphasized. The major problem is usually dust. If after processing your negatives are dried in a fairly dust-free situation, you will not have the problem of dust adhering to the surface of the film and becoming embedded while your negatives are drying. Dust that adheres to your film after it dries usually can be removed without too much difficulty.

Before you place the negative in the negative carrier, use a good sable-hair brush to remove dust from the surfaces of both sides of the frame you intend to enlarge. By holding the negative in a slant position under a direct light source (you can use the enlarger's light source for this), any dust specks that are present will readily be visible. Clean only the frame you intend to enlarge. If a brush is not available, use the small pinky of the hand that is not holding the negative to gently push aside any specks of dust lying on the surface of the film. Just be sure that your finger is perfectly dry before you touch the film. A large ear syringe can also be used to blow tiny specks of dust off your negative. In short, remember that spotless negatives produce spotless prints. With kids, however, our standards must be flexible.

After thoroughly cleaning your negative, place it in the enlarger. Turn on the enlarger and focus and compose the image on the easel. Focus carefully to be sure the image is sharp. In order to make focusing and framing easier, use a dummy sheet of enlarging paper in the easel. Compose and focus on the back of the paper.

The next step is the exposure of the image. Remove the dummy sheet of paper from the easel and replace it with a fresh piece of paper. There is a direct relationship between the density of your negative and the amount of light required for proper exposure. If your negative is thin, your exposure will require much less light than if your negative is dense.

The simplest way to determine the proper exposure for an enlargement is to make a test strip. A test strip is a series of exposures on a single sheet of paper using only one variable, say, the **time** of exposure. Turn on the enlarger and count 1,001, 1,002. Cover a section of the printing paper and count 1,001, 1,002 again. Make a series of such consistent increments using 1,001 and 1,002 as the time variable and progressively cover another section of the paper after each exposure. Try to do at least four or five steps. Process the paper as outlined below and look at the test strip under white light to determine the proper exposure. The section that looks best indicates the proper time of exposure.

After you've determined the proper time of exposure, place another sheet of enlarging paper in the easel and expose it for this amount of time. Slip your exposed paper into the developing tray and develop for a full two minutes while constantly agitating the solution in the tray. Remove the print from the developer, drain, and place it in the stop bath for 30 seconds. Remove, drain again, and place the print in a tray of fixer for eight minutes. Remember to agitate the print in each solution by rocking the tray. After fixing, wash the print for ten minutes in cold water. It is important to fill and dump the tray several times during the wash time. Then blot the print dry with paper toweling and allow it to air-dry face up on clean paper.

Making enlargements demands time and effort, but you should find that the results are well worth the trouble. With kids, it is important to emphasize cleanliness. After processing a print, have them dry their hands completely before handling the enlarger and negatives. Nothing can ruin equipment more quickly than a little acid fixer carelessly spread about the darkroom. Respect for equipment and materials is essential to good photographic practice.

The excitement and genuine enthusiasm generated by making enlargements is hard to believe. Kids get so engrossed in the procedures involved, that discipline is never in question. They seem to welcome whatever structure and organization is needed for the operation. The results are always fascinating.

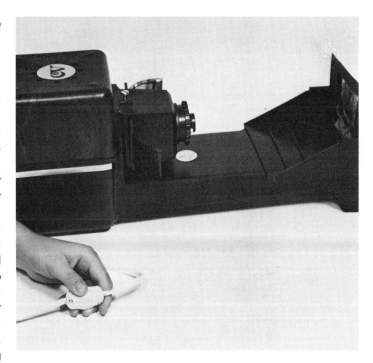

Make the exposure for the proper length of time.

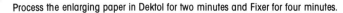

Process the enlarging paper in Dektol for two minutes and Fixer for four minutes.

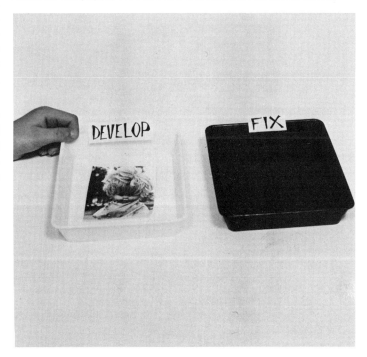

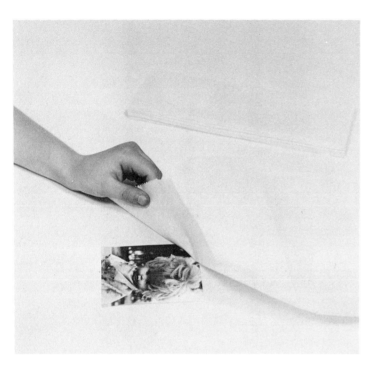

Wash and dry the print.

Here's the Instamatic negative enlarged.

Project 13:

Color Me Pink

Children generally prefer color images, but they will readily accept black-and-white ones once the cost and complexity of color processing is mentioned. Nevertheless, color is important to children and should be pursued in some form that is not too complicated or costly. This project is oriented toward the simpler uses of color, which can easily be added to any black-and-white print **after** processing.

You've already discovered how popular the color of P.O.P. is with children. The inherent, handsome brownish tones seem to harbor a certain mysterious charm that children simply can't resist. And, by adding a little common table salt to the fixer when processing P.O.P., you can turn the original reddish-brown color to deeper and deeper shades of chocolate brown, depending upon the amount of salt added (as mentioned in Project 1).

Color can dramatically alter the mood of a picture, and it doesn't have to be much color to effect a change. A pale green landscape or a pale blue seascape, for example, is always much more exciting to children than any plain, black-and-white print of the same image can ever be. Kids view black-and-white pictures as a bit too lackluster for their liking. They want to see their world as it is ... as it **really** is. If they can't have all of the glorious colors found in nature (or on color TV) in their prints, they'll certainly settle for just about any semblance of color you can provide.

The quickest way to establish color in a black-and-white picture is to soak it in a color bath. There are several color-producing household products that can be used for this purpose. Cranberry and grape juices, for example, are very practical coloring agents. Regular enlarging papers will soak up liquid color rather quickly. Do not use the new resin-coated papers, however, because the plastic coating prevents absorption of liquids into the body of the paper.

When coloring prints, remember that the soaking time is variable. Try 15 to 30 minutes as a starting point, but some colors may take upwards of one to two hours to achieve a desirable tone. Be sure to interleave the prints during the soaking operation. This helps avoid staining and ensures an even coloration. Experimenting with the soaking time is the best way to discover what different coloring agents will do.

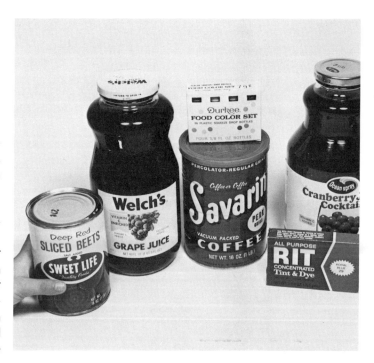

Shown here are some ordinary household items suitable for coloring photos: beet, grape, and cranberry juices, coffee, and fabric dyes.

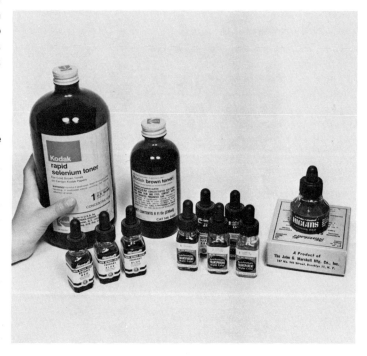

Some photo supply store items suitable for coloring photos: selenium toner, brown toner, photo retouch colors, liquid water colors, colored inks, and tube colors.

Soak the print in a tray until the desired color quality is obtained.

Wash and dry the print as usual.

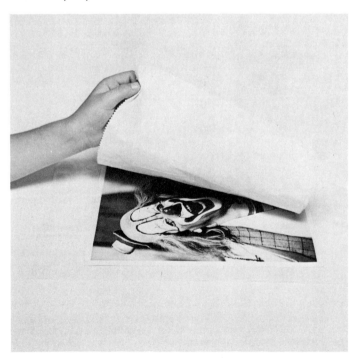

There is one coloring agent that is really something special. Keep that old, stale coffee left over from breakfast. It's quite a miracle worker. Kids are often more impressed with the sepia tones produced from coffee baths than with the colors achieved by practically any other means. Those coffee-soaked "black-and-whites" really look archaic. Almost any picture takes on the "vintage" look of many of those venerable old-time photos found in grandma's attic. Yes, the kids could almost fool the experts into believing that their coffee-stained Diana pictures are original Victorian images.

Most supermarkets carry several brand-name, all-purpose dyes used by the modern homemaker. Available both in powder and liquid form, they furnish lots of controllable color at a modest price. It is advisable to use rubber or plastic gloves whenever you employ synthetic dyes. Cover work areas carefully with newspapers and, of course, use protective clothing. These precautions are especially important when working with enthusiastic youngsters.

In some cases, you may want to protect the container itself (dishpan, tray, etc.) from discoloration. This can easily be accomplished by spreading a thin, protective coating of petroleum jelly (Vaseline) over the entire surface of the container. When the drying operation is complete, the jelly can be removed with soap and warm water.

For those of you who may prefer to use some of the more conventional photocoloring methods, try a few of the commercial products from your local camera shop. Kodak Blue Toner and Brown Toner are both liquids. Mixed according to directions, they serve as soak baths very similar to the above, but each produces its own distinctive coloration. Unlike some of the household products mentioned earlier, these solutions do work with resin-coated papers. The results are not equal to those attained with the more traditional papers, but definite tonal colorations are visible.

There are other makes of commercial toning agents that you may wish to try. GAF makes Liquid Flemish, Direct Sepia, and Vivitoner. Edwal produces a series of single-solution toners—blue, green, yellow, red, and brown; other colors can be obtained by toning the same print successively in different solutions.

As an alternative to the soak-bath method, try coloring pictures by applying color directly to the surface of the print with a brush. In this way, you can apply different colors to separate areas of the picture to produce a multicolored image. Enlarging papers with matte surfaces work best for this procedure, but glossy papers can also be used provided you are not fussy about the results. Edwal Foto Tint colors take well to black-and-white prints, are water soluble for easy cleanup, and are permanent once applied to the paper. Colors available are red, yellow, orange, blue, brown, violet, amber, green, gray, olive, magenta, and cyan. They come in a set of 12 one-ounce bottles or may be purchased individually. Kodak and Marshall offer photo retouch colors that can be used for the same purpose. Some art shops carry the half-ounce bottles of Dr. Martin's liquid dyes, which are also suitable for hand coloring prints.

When applying color directly to the surface of a print, be sure to work up solutions in small areas at a time. Care must be taken so that puddles of color do not form on the print's surface, or rings and uneven results will occur. The technique is a slow and meticulous process, but the results are well worth the effort. You can either duplicate the normal colors of a scene, or indulge in some of the wildest color you might wish to conjure up.

One more color twist that's a lot of fun to try is using the pastel-type paper, which employs a color rather than a white paper base. These papers are used in the same manner as any other black-and-white paper; the only difference is that the black image comes up on a color background instead of a white one. The choice of colors is red, blue, green, yellow, gold, and silver. Pastel papers are marketed by several companies—Luminos Photo Corp., Spiratone Inc., and Delta Import/Distribution. This last company markets the product under the brand name of Argenta. (For addresses of these companies, see the "Sources and Resources" section of this book.)

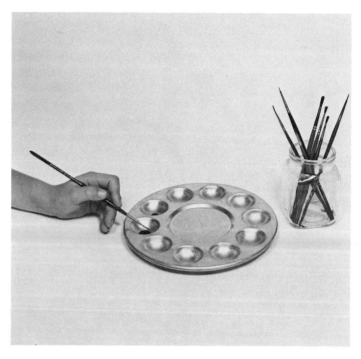

An artist's palette is helpful when hand coloring the prints. Use 00 sable brushes and color only a small section of the print at a time.

A spray finish is good protection for the colored prints.

Cranberry juice would make an excellent color for this clown (pink to red).

Project 14:

Instant Slides

How would you like a quick and easy way of producing large pictures from small negatives without all the fuss and bother of making enlargements? Yea! Yea! Actually, you may even have a hankering to try 35mm or some other small-format film with kids. However, you know only too well that small negatives must really be enlarged to be appreciated, and that's one hassle you just aren't about to get yourself into.

Instafilm to the rescue! All you have to do is take any small negative, make a quick contact print on a piece of Instafilm, apply a little magic heat, and you're ready to gloat over your picture-taking efforts. You can now project that picture, as big as life, on any screen or nearby wall. Sounds easy? Well, it is. Better still, you don't even need a darkroom to do it!

Starex, Inc. sells a complete 60-second slide kit for $16.50. Packed in a sturdy, white box, you'll find a 25-foot roll of Instafilm, 100 2″ × 2″ Quick-Mounts, six plastic and glass printing frames, three 35mm-length guides, a pair of cotton gloves, film tweezers, a pad of bond paper, lens tissue, a lint-free cleaning cloth, and a step-by-step instruction booklet.

Instafilm has really been around for some time! Manufactured by Metro/Kalvar Inc., it is used primarily as a dry photographic duplicating system. Its major applications are in the motion picture, television, and educational firm industries. The system is based on a light-scattering principle within a film of thermoplastic, resin coated on a transparent polyester base. Conventional silver halide materials, on the other hand, are activated by a light-absorption phenomenon.

The film is sensitive primarily to the ultraviolet side of the light spectrum, which makes it comparatively safe to use under ordinary levels of visible light (and an ideal material to use with kids). Exposure is accomplished in one of three ways—with a 300- or 500-watt fan-cooled slide projector, with sunlight, or with special ultraviolet lamps (sunlamps, mercury-vapor arc lamps, carbon arc lamps, and so forth). The slide projector method is obviously tailor-made to meet our needs, and this is what the Starex system is based upon.

Buying the film directly from the manufacturer is possible, but you must purchase it in bulk quantities. Starex

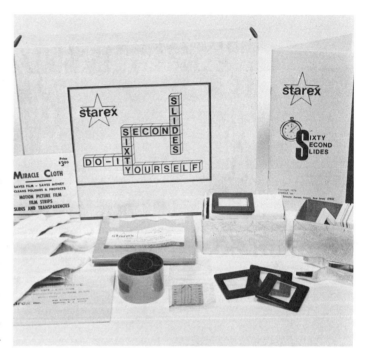

The complete Starex Do-It-Yourself Instant Slide Kit contains: Instafilm, 2″ × 2″ Quick-Mounts, print frames, 35mm-length guides, cotton gloves, film tweezers, bond paper, lens tissue, lint-free cleaning cloth, and a step-by-step instruction booklet.

Place the negative to be printed in the white half of a glass slide binder with the dull emulsion side up.

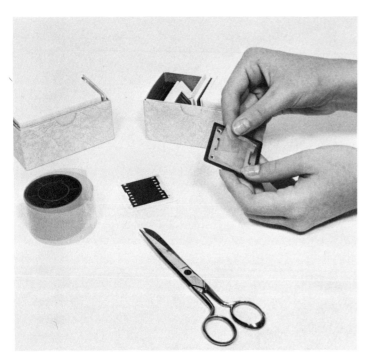

Place the previously cut Instafilm in the gray half of the glass slide binder with the emulsion side up.

Tightly close the two parts of the slide binder. The emulsion sides of both pieces of film are facing each other.

will sell the film and/or any other part of the slide kit separately. A 25-foot roll of Instafilm sells for $3.85, and the step-by-step instruction booklet is $1. You should also be able to buy Instafilm from your local audiovisual supply house, or they should at least be able to tell you about some other retail outlet where the film is available.

Working with Instafilm is pure joy—a simple 1-2-3 process.

1. Place the negative to be copied with a piece of Instafilm into any double-glass slide binder.

2. Insert the loaded slide binder into any 300- or 500-watt slide projector and expose.

3. Remove and apply moderate heat to the exposed piece of Instafilm, and presto, the image appears as if by magic.

It's as easy as that. Now you can project the finished image and enjoy the results of your picture-taking efforts.

Exposure time is variable, depending on the density of the original negative and the bulb wattage of the projector employed. The Starex exposure table included in their instruction booklet provides a good starting point for individual testing of the Instafilm material. With very little trial and error, you should quickly discover the correct exposure time required to produce excellent results with your specific negative/projector combination. A 500-watt slide projector might require a slightly shorter exposure time, while a 250-watt projector might require a slightly longer exposure time. Remember that reds and browns in color films may necessitate longer exposures. Image results that are too light come from underexposure. Likewise, dark images come from overexposure. Heavy, grainy images are due to overdevelopment or from the grain in the original negative or slide.

Developing Instafilm is simplicity itself. After exposure, separate the piece of Instafilm from the negative in the slide binder. Place the exposed piece of Instafilm (emulsion side down) between two sheets of ordinary white bond paper and apply moderate heat with a flat-iron. Be sure to preheat the iron to the correct temperature by setting the controls for low or synthetic fabrics. Place the moderately heated flatiron over the film and paper sandwich and lightly apply pressure with a quick, rotary motion for approximately one to two seconds. Remove the developed Instafilm from the paper sandwich, insert it into any slide mount, and project. The green tint, which is characteristic of the film, will disappear in a few seconds.

Once fully developed, Instafilm will last for years. Since it's made with a polyester base, it will not tear, split, or break. This makes Instafilm very tolerant to the kind of rough handling that little hands can give it. In fact, you

Insert the glass slide binder into the projector slot with the original negative (the white half) closest to the light source.

Turn on the projector and expose the negative for the designated time.

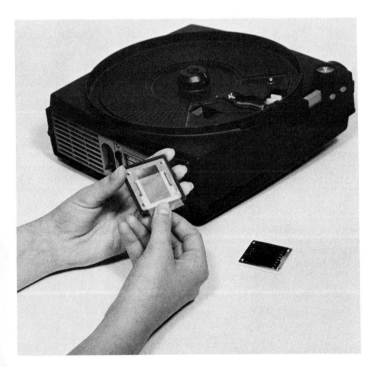

Remove the exposed Instafilm from the slide binder.

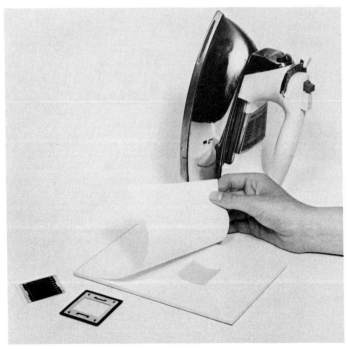

Place the Instafilm between two sheets of lint-less paper, then apply an iron (set for low) to the film/paper sandwich and rotate it lightly for one or two seconds.

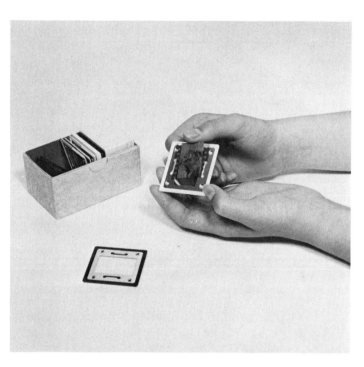

Remove the film after developing and insert it into any slide mount.

must use scissors to cut it. (Adults may wish to use an X-Acto knife or a razor blade.)

The advantages of Instafilm are indeed plentiful, especially in the teaching of photography to kids. Besides the fact that the film is practically indestructible, its ultraviolet light sensitivity means that it is reasonably safe to handle under most normal room lighting conditions. Obviously, Instafilm must be kept away from direct sunlight, and it is also advisable to minimize its exposure to fluorescent lighting if you are in a school situation. Still, this is a far cry from the requirements of darkroom conditions. Since low levels of visible light have no effect on unexposed Instafilm, it can be handled freely without a darkroom until the moment of exposure. It is advisable to keep the unused portion of Instafilm in the original lightproof pouch.

Speaking of the darkroom, Instafilm is not called a "Space Age Miracle" for nothing. It not only evades the whole darkroom scene in terms of film handling, but also in terms of film development. No chemical processing of this film occurs at any stage of the slide-making procedure; it is developed by heat alone.

One thing that is most important to consider when using Instafilm, however, is the whole question of dust removal. Be extremely careful of dust and lint! If not removed prior to exposure, dust will show up as white spots and lint as white curlicues on the screen. Check each side of the glass slide binder, the negative, and the Instafilm itself before exposure. A bit of serious scrutiny before exposure can save lots of film later.

A few more points should be mentioned. If the projector you are using produces a "hot spot" of gray in the center of the duplicate prior to the completion of the exposure time, the projector's cooling system is inadequate. This is a result of too much heat, which starts film development too soon. Cut down your exposure time or use another projector. With silver halide films, the emulsion side is the dull side. With Instafilm, the emulsion side is the side that curls up at the edges.

Instafilm provides you with the means of quickly turning any black-and-white or color negatives into black-and-white positives. You can also print color transparencies on Instafilm to produce black-and-white negatives, which in turn can be reprinted on Instafilm to make black-and-white positives of your original color slides. A versatile medium indeed! Any classroom teacher can take a 35mm or Instamatic camera to school and build a whole photography program around Instafilm. Of course, if you use an Instamatic negative instead of a 35mm negative, use Instamatic-type double-glass slide binders to make prints or duplicates on Instafilm. You can use these in any 35mm slide projector.

By the way, Instafilm is also produced in sheet size. Just imagine what you could do with that! Lantern slide projector, let there be a carnival of light. Color can be added to Instafilm by using a transparent adhesive color material (sold in most art shops) or by using transparent permanent markers such as those made by Starex (LUMO-4S). A more modest monochrome effect (sepia) can be achieved by using a low temperature setting (below 250 F) on the flatiron when developing Instafilm. Instant slide is an old twist to some new fun and is highly recommended for a rainy day at home with the kids.

Project the Instaslide on a screen or a white wall. The green tint will disappear after a few seconds.

The projected slide is shown here.

Project 15:

Photomontage

It was in Dessau, Germany, that a group of prominent artists gathered to form a school for artists and designers that would revolutionize visual-arts education in its time. This school, better known as the Bauhaus, quickly evolved into a great center for visual-arts experimentation. The Bauhaus was thus responsible for ushering in a period of visual exploration and discovery that has reverberated throughout each generation of artists and designers since its inception in the 1920's.

Laszlo Moholy-Nagy, one of the founders of the Bauhaus movement, began to utilize the photographic image as an abstract device capable of producing a nonliteral visual statement. He and Man Ray were among the first to revitalize the old-fashioned photogram process. The photogram is a technique in which photographic images are created directly by placing opaque or translucent objects on a sheet of photographic paper and exposing them to a light source.

Moholy-Nagy originated many of the darkroom manipulations that he employed in his work. Such techniques as double exposure, double printing, combination negatives, and montage provided the foundations for a new vocabulary in the photographic medium. The last technique mentioned is undoubtedly one of the most interesting manipulative devices used in photography. Peter Pollack states in his massive volume **The Picture History of Photography** that it was Moholy-Nagy who "reawakened artistic interest in photomontage, often adding fanciful touches and Surrealist incongruities."

The line of demarcation between "collage" and "montage" is often blurred. For the sake of delineation, a montage is constructed primarily in terms of photographic elements, while a collage is virtually unrestricted in its use of visual components. Montage enables the photographer to reconstruct his photographic images into new visual forms, and unlike collage, it is distinctly photographic in technique.

Though photomontage is somewhat more defined as a medium than collage, there is still a considerable margin for devising individualized techniques. This writer produces a photomontage by adhering premounted and precut photographic elements onto a permanent plywood panel. This operation can be divided into six progressive steps.

Select a series of related photographs.

Dry mount the pictures onto thin pieces of mat board.

Cut the pictures into desired sections.

1. A series of related photographs are taken on negative film.

2. The pictures are processed and printed on a high-contrast paper, say, Ilford number five or, even better, Agfa number six.

3. The prints are dried and dry mounted to pieces of thin mat board.

4. The prints are trimmed and cut into various pieces.

5. The resulting elements are laid out on a flat surface and organized into a pattern or design; they can also be numbered consecutively once their permanent order is determined.

6. The last and most important step in the process is to adhere said photographic elements securely to the plywood panel, which is the support for the finished montage. An epoxy-type cement is probably the most reliable adhesive for this purpose, but a white cream glue is sufficient. The montage can easily be framed by facing the edges of the panel with a thin stripping of prepainted wood.

Selecting the visual material for the series of photographs that will eventually be organized into a montage is one of the most important steps in the technique. The pho-

tographer must plan the relationship of his photographs in advance. The necessity of working with a theme or motif in mind is basic to the success or failure of the montage, since the photographer cannot predict the exact visual outcome of his work. By selecting and utilizing a theme or motif, the family of pictorial elements that emerges will provide the montage with the analogous components necessary for coherence. In short, the photographer can and does insure himself of probable success by the manner in which he creates the elements that will eventually form the finished montage.

The choice of a high-contrast photographic printing paper has been determined by this writer's decision to limit himself to the extremes of the black-and-white scale. Thus, many of the gray values are omitted in order to emphasize the abstract potentialities of the montage medium. By printing on extra-hard photographic paper, the photographer can produce graphic results that are ideally suited to the characteristic visual synthesis of montage. Full-scale prints, however, can also be quite effective.

Montage offers an interesting method of reevaluating and synthesizing visual experience. By cutting the series of photographs into assorted pieces, the photographer is compelled to reevaluate the visual material in the light of the new elements that are created. This assortment of pieces provides the photographer with an opportunity to reassemble the disconnected elements into a new, coherent, visual whole—the montage. The final organization of elements should foster a visual synthesis that results in an entirely **new** visual experience.

Use heavy books to hold the elements flat until dry.

Lay out the resulting elements on a flat surface and organize them into a pattern or design (far left).

Apply adhesive to the back of each element and press each one onto the plywood (left).

Frame the montage by facing the edges of the panel with thin strippings of prepainted wood (right).

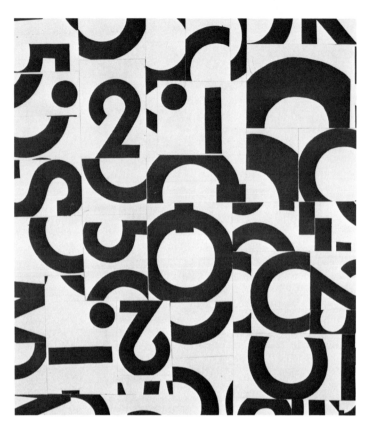

Here's the finished montage. Note the interesting contrast.

Different poses of the same person make a nice pattern.

Project 16:

The Paper Negative

Eager to try photography with grade school children, but find cost the major drawback? Here is a simple introduction to a medium that can be attempted in any room that can be darkened temporarily. The cost is negligible; needed are a piece of heavy plate glass (or a printing frame), a floodlight, a few chemicals, some photographic paper, a dozen clean white blotters, and you're in business.

This particular technique is based on the paper negative process so common in the graphic-arts trade. A negative can be made on photosensitive paper as well as on photosensitive film. In the photocopy process, a thin paper-base photoemulsion material (something like a lightweight enlarging paper) is used directly in the large process camera to make paper negatives. This paper negative is then printed in direct contact with photographic paper to obtain a positive print. Most architectural drawings and renderings are usually reproduced by this method. It is simple, highly effective, and less expensive than a film-base medium.

A good substitute for the paper negative is the paper positive, which can easily be obtained from any current newspaper or magazine. The images in these periodicals are printed on a paper that is thin enough to be reprinted on regular photographic paper. The only drawback in using pictures from newspapers or magazines is that they produce an automatic double image because every page in a newspaper or magazine has printed matter on both sides of the page. This apparent disadvantage can be turned into profitable gain by taking advantage of the subtleties offered by the double image.

Selecting double images that offer printing potential from newspapers and magazines can be quite intriguing. When searching for suitable image material, the page should be viewed against a bright light source such as a window in daylight or a lamp shade with the light on so that the images appear transparent. In this way, an approximation of the finished product can be pre-visualized. Remember that the finished print will be **negative.** This means that all the tones in the picture selected will be reversed.

Selecting the potential images is first done visually, by looking at the front and back of each page and anticipating the product.

Carefully cut the page selected to make sure that the potential image is not destroyed.

Examine the page for picture potential by holding it against a window. A general outline of the double image is readily visible.

In the darkroom, place the page over a piece of enlarging paper, cover with glass, and expose to light for 30 seconds.

Process the paper as usual: Dektol—two minutes, Fixer—four minutes.

Wash and dry the product as usual.

The printing materials for this type of photographic endeavor are minimal. Prerequisite, of course, is again a small room that can be made completely dark; a closet will do nicely. Also needed is a printing frame, which can be simulated with a piece of 8″ × 10″ plate glass from your local glazier. If you're going to use ordinary window glass, it should be heavy enough to hold down a piece of photographic paper and the selected image so that both are completely flat. A floodlight or a plain, bare bulb hanging from an electric cord will provide an effective light source.

The photographic chemicals used for this process are paper developer, rapid fixer, and hypo eliminator (optional). The 8″ × 10″ (single-weight glossy) photographic paper can be purchased in a package of 25 sheets or a box of 100 sheets. Photographic blotters are available in roll form with a corrugated core or in cut sheet form.

The process is simple. First, select the image to be used. Place this image on a sheet of photographic paper (shiny side up) under the plate glass. Expose the whole sandwich to light for approximately 30 seconds. Develop the photographic paper for two minutes. (Any red bulb can be used as a safelight if you prefer not working in the dark; photographic paper is not sensitive to red light.) After developing, place the paper in a water bath for about 15 seconds to stop the developing. Then place the paper in the rapid fixer for four minutes and in the hypo eliminator for two minutes (if used).

Judge the print under white light. If the print is too dark, **reduce** the exposure. If the print is too light, **increase** the exposure. The ideal exposure can easily be discovered by trial and error. Or if you prefer, use the test-strip method outlined in Project 12.

Keep all prints in a water tray until all the printing you'll be doing is finished. (Resin-coated papers must be washed and dried immediately; soaking is harmful to them.) Wash the final prints in running water, emptying the tray completely at regular intervals for fifteen minutes. (Resin-coated papers demand a much shorter wash time, usually no more than four minutes.) Sponge or squeegee the excess water from each of the prints and place them between (or on top of for resin-coated papers) blotters to dry overnight.

The reverse image can be printed by placing the product over another sheet of enlarging paper, covering it with glass, and exposing it for one to two minutes.

Here's the negative image of the exposed original (right).

There is something exciting about the double image. It seems to evoke a sense of mystery and wonder. It invites the viewer to create his own meaning—to project and conceive within the limits of a given context. Searching through the printed pages of newspapers and magazines for appropriate picture material provides kids with an excellent opportunity to previsualize and conceptualize. Kids are forced to create meaning out of images that are superimposed by virtue of the fact that they fall on opposite sides of the same page. The challenge is formidable. The images that result are most fascinating.

When printing a page from a magazine or a newspaper, the image that results is **negative**. This image, however, may also be printed on another sheet of enlarging paper, and then a positive image will result. It's fun to see how some images are much more interesting in the negative and others in the positive. Experiment and see what you like.

This is the positive image of the exposed original.

Project 17:

X-Raygrams

You don't want to bother with buying a camera? Then why not print some "ready-made" negatives? After a certain period of time, medical X-ray labs often discard old X-rays as a matter of course. Even in the case of X-rays, storage space is a problem. So every once in a while, a housecleaning is in order and out go batches of unserviceable X-rays.

To the unsuspecting eye, X-rays would seem to have little value other than their immediate medical application. But to the student of photography, they represent a fascinating avenue of visual exploration. X-rays, combined with a few packages of photosensitive paper, can provide hours of graphic discovery for kids and adults alike.

Few materials are necessary. However, a small room or closet that can be darkened is essential. An X-ray cache can often be procured from any hospital center or from one's local radiologist. Ask! It is surprising what may be available. Aside from the discarded X-rays and a dark closet or darkroom, all the materials are available wherever photo supplies are sold. The photo counter in a local discount store often carries many brand-name materials at reduced costs. Why pay retail prices when you can get the same items at a discount? In photography, expense is a factor that can be greatly minimized with a little effort and some shopping acumen.

Two lights are important in the "darkroom"—a white light for exposure of the paper and a filtered light so you can see what you are doing. Both lights can emanate from one source, since they do not have to be used simultaneously. In fact, even electricity is not a necessity. A heavy-duty flashlight will do. You can produce your own safelight/exposure source out of any ordinary store-bought flashlight. First, cut a Kodak No. 1 gelatin filter to fit the size of the glass in the front of the flashlight. Then insert this filter between the glass and the silver reflector inside the face of the light. When you're ready to make the "white-light" exposure, simply remove the filter from the face of the flashlight and expose accordingly.

The same basic approach can be used with an ordinary Kodak bullet safelight attached to an electric drop-cord socket. The filter recommended by Kodak for enlarging papers is the AO series. (The red 1A filter would

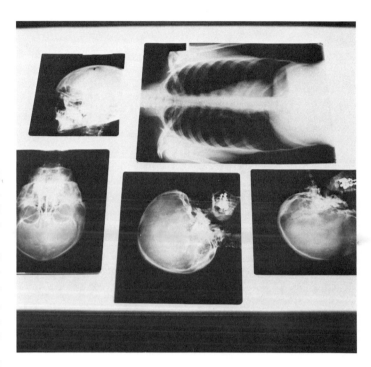

Collect X-rays and examine them for visual potential.

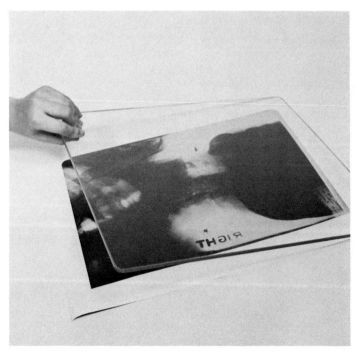

Select the X-ray to be printed, place it over the enlarging paper, and cover it with glass.

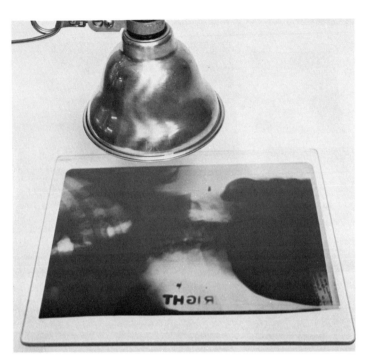

Expose the X-ray to white light for one to two minutes.

work just as well.) It should be used with no more than a 15-watt bulb. Use the same flashlight without the filter for exposing the paper.

The photographic paper employed can be either regular enlarging paper or the resin-coated variety. Resin-coated papers are easier to wash and dry than regular papers. Only two chemicals are necessary—Dektol (a paper developer) and Rapid Fixer (a good all-round fixing agent). Both of these chemicals were mentioned in past projects where mixing and storage procedures were explained. Other than a few trays (glass or plastic) and a piece of windowpane glass (cut to the size of the paper to be used), a little creativity is all that is needed to bring about fascinating graphic results.

First, select an X-ray on the basis of its visual potential. Place the X-ray over a piece of enlarging paper and cover with a sheet of clean glass. Expose the sandwich to white light, and develop the exposed paper in Dektol for a full two minutes. Rinse the print in a water bath for ten seconds, and then immerse it in Rapid Fixer for four minutes.

It is important to understand the sandwich procedure. The paper, which is on the bottom of the sandwich, should be placed emulsion side up toward the light source. The emulsion side of the paper is the shiny side. The X-ray

Process the paper in Dektol—two minutes; Fixer—four minutes.

Wash and dry the paper as usual.

also has an emulsion side, and it should be facing down so as to come in contact with the emulsion side of the paper. The emulsion side of the X-ray is the dull side. Though the paper must always be placed in the sandwich emulsion side up, the X-ray need not always be, depending upon the effects sought. The glass cover in the sandwich helps insure better contact between the X-ray and the enlarging paper.

In order to minimize the trial and error involved in finding the proper exposure for a particular sandwich setup, you should make a "test strip." Instead of using a full sheet of enlarging paper in the sandwich, use only a third of a sheet in the setup. Then expose the entire sandwich to white light for five seconds. Follow this procedure at one-inch intervals until the entire strip of enlarging paper is exposed. Process the strip in the usual manner and then examine it under white light. The strip should have approximately six to eight steps across its surface, each having a different exposure at five-second increments. Determine the best exposure and add five seconds for each step up to the one selected. For example, say the fourth step seems to be the best exposure of the set; count across the test strip four steps, adding five seconds each time. Thus, 20 seconds would be the correct exposure.

Set up the sandwich again. Expose a full sheet of

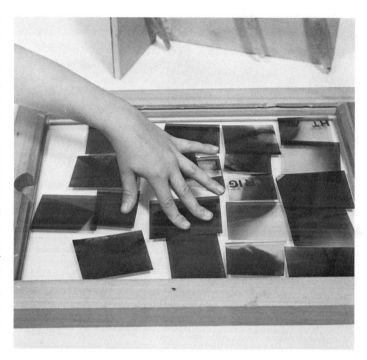

The printing of cut-up X-rays is much easier if a print frame is used. Arrange the sections of the X-rays on the glass of the frame, then cover with enlarging paper (emulsion side down), and expose them as usual.

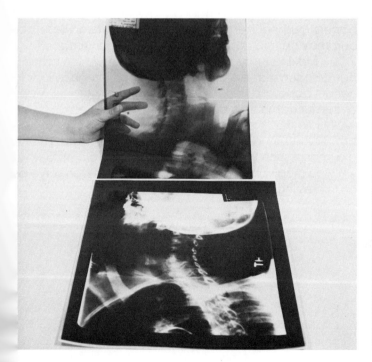

The X-ray and the product held side by side.

As an interesting variation, cut the X-rays into sections and rearrange the parts to make a suitable visual design.

Here's the product of the cut-up X-ray technique.

enlarging paper for 20 seconds and process accordingly. Voilà! The final print appears. The test-strip method of selecting the proper exposure is really one of the most expedient ways to determine exposure.

Once the student gets the knack of the procedure, he or she can then experiment more freely, exploring the possibilities of the materials involved. An X-ray can be cut up and its parts rearranged. The student can use the "flop-negative" technique, printing only half of the sandwich at a time, then reversing the X-ray or flopping it over so as to print the same image on the other side. Sections of the X-ray can even be painted out or designs scratched in, graffiti style. The possibilities are limited only by one's ingenuity.

Once you've made all the prints you want to make, wash them thoroughly in running water. If you would like to cut down on the wash time, first use Kodak Hypo Clearing Agent, Perma Wash, or any suitable hypo eliminator. This will reduce the wash time considerably. Of course when using resin-coated papers, eliminators are not required.

After the prints are washed, they must be dried. They should be placed face down on a flat, smooth surface such as an aluminum cookie sheet or a Formica counter top and rolled with a brayer to remove much of the excess water prior to drying. A squeegee may also be used. Then place the prints between clean photographic blotters and leave them to dry overnight. Resin-coated papers must not be placed between blotters. These papers may be laid out to air-dry on any clean surface.

Making X-raygrams can be a lot of fun. The process can also serve as an inexpensive way to introduce kids to certain basic aspects of the photographic process. Many of the fundamentals of photography can be woven directly into the X-raygram project. After all, Henry Fox Talbot (1800-1877) did not have X-rays to work with, but he did imprint such things as lace and leaves to create what we would call photograms. The X-raygrams can serve as an interesting variation of this idea.

Project 18:

Image Ingenuity

As we've seen in the last few projects, you don't need to buy an expensive camera to make exciting pictures. In fact, you don't need a camera at all. Simply purchase two sheets of ordinary window glass, sprinkle them with a little ingenuity, and presto, you have the potential for making lots of photographic images.

Take one sheet of window glass, pour any gooey substance that has some density (like blackstrap molasses) onto it, press a second sheet of glass on top, and suddenly you have an instant design. Place this same sandwich over a sheet of photographic paper, expose it to a light bulb, and process normally. The results are fascinating. Actually, anything translucent can be pressed between glass and printed in the same way. Try using one sheet of ordinary window glass and topping it with a heavy sheet of plate glass cut to the same size. This gizmo will allow you to print just about anything that light can pass through. You're limited only by your imagination.

If you are fortunate enough to have access to a darkroom that has an enlarger, you're really in business. Replace the negative carrier in the enlarger with two smaller sheets of glass, hinged together on one side with tape. Now you can not only make designs in this glass sandwich, but you can also enlarge them. Enlarging can produce peculiar designs with the most inconspicuous images and effects.

Many interesting images, for example, can be created by placing several layers of cellophane tape on the glass and scorching it with a match. You can also try placing various substances between glass and heating parts of the sandwich with a small flame, like a cigarette lighter or a Bunsen burner.

Having exhausted the various materials at hand, you can collect pieces of broken 8mm or 16mm film or old 35mm film strips. (If you're a teacher, it pays to be friendly with your media specialist.) Place whole sections of these film images between glass, enlarge, and voilà—instant Andy Warhol. Take a small section of film and try making some extreme blowups by projecting images onto enlarging paper that is placed on the floor.

Making images without a camera can be fun, especially if you're short of funds. Providing you can develop some kind of makeshift darkroom, there is no limit to

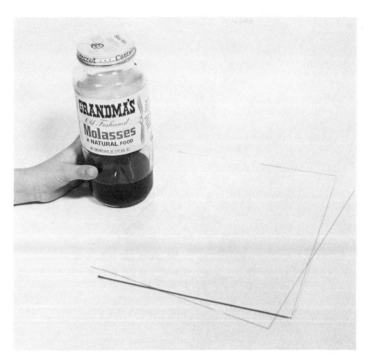

Old-fashioned molasses can be pressed between two sheets of window glass to produce interesting results.

This is a fabricated hinged glass carrier for the enlarger.

To use the monoprinting technique, draw, paint, or whatever on a sheet of 8″ × 10″ glass, cover with a clean sheet of ordinary typing paper, and rub the entire surface of the paper with your fingers. Remove the sheet of paper starting at one corner and allow it to dry. Place the completed monoprint over a sheet of enlarging paper, cover it with glass, and expose it to white light for one minute.

Printing leaves, weeds, doilies, is easy when using a piece of heavy plate glass.

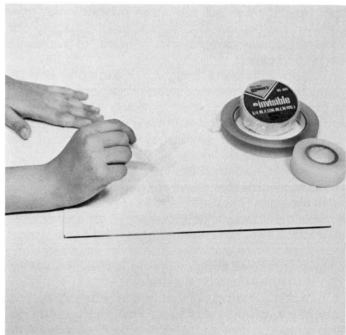

the images that you can produce simply by using a few sheets of glass and making contact-type prints. If you have ready access to an enlarger, you can really experiment.

You can make many kinds of images without a camera. The process outlined here is definitely open-ended. Think of the possibilities of using many of the techniques employed in a more primitive printing process like monoprinting. On a single 8" × 10" sheet of glass, you can draw, paint, print, make a collage, or whatever. As long as the image is partially translucent, it **will print.** Check your local library for art books that explain the basic techniques of monoprinting. You'll be surprised what will print; all you have to do is place the product atop some enlarging paper, pass light through it, and a photographic print will result.

In using the monoprinting concepts, you should use plate glass. It is heavier than common window glass, and its added weight will hold the photographic paper flat for the printing exposure. Tracing paper is ideal for making drawings of all kinds and transferring them to photographic paper. Place the tracing paper directly over the photographic paper and use the sheet of plate glass to hold the whole sandwich together.

Anything that will print can be turned into a photo image. The only prerequisite is that the material to be printed should be translucent enough to allow light to pass through. Some opaque materials may be printed, providing light can pass through certain sections of the object to furnish printable results (for example, doilies, tatting, and lace). The camera can sometimes be more of a hindrance than a help for making certain kinds of imagery. Using the little box with a hole is only one way of making photo images. A whole world in photography can be pursued without ever using a camera. So don't let a little thing like a camera stand between you and some really fascinating photographic images.

White cream glue produces many different degrees of opacity.

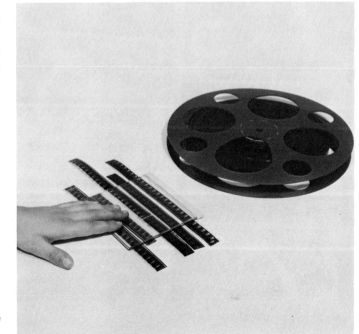

Motor grease on glass can produce some fine designs (far left).

Transparent tape can be layered to produce interesting patterns (left).

Old 16mm film clips used in a glass frame for an enlargement can produce some fascinating Pop Art effects (right).

Here's the result using the 16mm film clips.

Project 19:

Projectograms

Making projectograms is an inexpensive and exciting alternative to the many negative–positive approaches to photography already presented. Projecting gigantic abstractions many times larger than anything children can create on paper is especially attractive to them. The materials are few and the possibilities are many. All that is really needed is some sort of slide projector; everything else should be easy enough to acquire.

Many people have their own 35mm slide projectors, and most schools should be able to provide not only a 35mm projector, but also a 3¼″ × 4″ lantern slide projector, a 2¼″ × 2¼″ slide projector, a filmstrip projector, and even an overhead projector. In any case, any one of these machines is suitable transit for your journey into that giant wonderland of projected visual fabrications.

Starting with a few sheets of clear, transparent acetate (available from your local art supply store), a box of cardboard slide mounts, and a couple of waterproof felt markers, you can create a carnival-like atmosphere of projected colors. Just cut pieces of clear acetate to fit the slide mounts, draw on the acetate with the markers, affix the cardboard mount, and project. Simple as that!

As a variant, you may wish to try slide cover glass. Sold at your local photo dealer in several sizes ranging from 2″ × 2″ to 3¼″ × 4″, they are excellent for making transparency sandwiches. Any transparent or translucent material may be "sandwiched" between two pieces of slide cover glass, taped on at least two sides, and projected. A special slide tape is manufactured for this purpose, but you can also use plastic, transparent, or masking tape, whichever is handy.

Instead of tape, try spreading a thin layer of petroleum jelly on one side of each slide cover glass. Then apply transparent material right over the jelly. Press the pieces of glass together, jelly to jelly, and they stick together just like magic—no tape is necessary! Most of the time, the making of slide sandwiches is a temporary affair used primarily for experimental purposes. So a few pieces of slide cover glass can go a long way. After the children are finished exploring and investigating the possibilities of the sandwich medium, a little cleaning will make each piece of slide cover glass as good as new.

If you would like to make sandwich transparencies

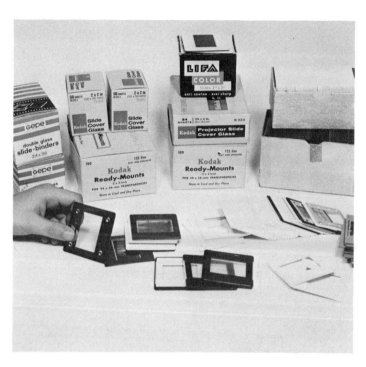

There are many types of slide mounts on the market: cardboard, plastic, glass, and a variety of plastic-and-glass combinations.

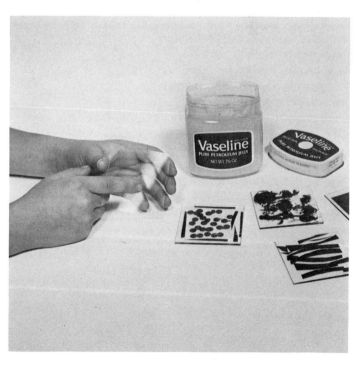

Spread a thin layer of petroleum jelly on the inner face of each slide cover glass to hold the slide together. Transparency materials are applied directly over the jelly.

Tabletop guide in the "U"FILM kit sets off three filmstrip frames at a time to keep your task in perspective. Two filmstrip frames are equal to one 35mm slide frame.

Almost any kind of drawing material can be used to create your giant designs on "U"FILM.

with little children but fear cuts from broken glass, use Plexiglas (as mentioned in Project 3). Glass mounts embedded in plastic frames are also suitable for this purpose. Though a bit more expensive than plain glass, they too are completely reusable.

Another material that's fun to use is a product called "U"FILM. With "U"FILM, you can make full-color slides (or filmstrips) as easily as you can write your name. There's no camera, no darkroom, and no chemical fuss.

"U"FILM is a tough plastic film material that is exactly the size of standard 35mm perforated film. Instead of utilizing a normal, photographic emulsion on the film base, the manufacturer has created a specially treated blank surface upon which you can write, draw, paint, type, and even apply certain opaque or transparent materials. Since "U"FILM can easily be erased, it is completely reusable. When a slide or a filmstrip is no longer needed, it can quickly be reclaimed by washing. The film can also be sprayed with certain fixatives for greater protection and durability. Spraying with a fixative prevents smudging or accidental erasure of the finished product. Even most fixatives can be removed with the proper solvents should you later decide that you want to salvage a piece of "U"FILM.

Don't worry about your ability to draw. Since the frame area to be projected is very small, the tiny image is quite abstract when it appears on the screen. A few swabs of color across a frame become a whole painting when projected. If you would like to combine color with some typed material, apply the color to the film before you put it in the typewriter.

You must always use the dull side of "U"FILM for any writing, drawing, painting, and so forth. The dull side will accept most surface treatments. You can use pencil, pen and ink, crayon, felt-tip marker, watercolor, and even rub-on lettering. All these materials, however, perform with varying degrees of success. You must select the particular materials that will give you the results you are looking for. When you use color, you should always start with the lightest color and proceed to the darkest, otherwise the dark color will smudge when you apply the lighter color.

"U"FILM's forte and true potential seems to really come to flower when it is applied to purely creative ends. Like Norman McLaren, the famous Canadian film animator who paints and draws directly on clear 35mm film base, your kids can create lively, full-color slide series and filmstrip sequences that can actually become "projected art."

By applying splotches of color, simple drawings, and various abstract designs made with water-soluble art materials directly onto the dull side of "U"FILM, kids can create a panorama of visual possibilities. Detailed work is not even recommended, for the movement of color and form itself should be emphasized.

After you've finished a slide series or a filmstrip, darken the room for "the show must go on" to be really appreciated. The effect produced by combining "U"FILM's specially treated film base with the various art materials that are applied to its surface is quite startling when projected. It has a very unusual quality all its own. The overall grain inherent in the specially treated film base seems to enhance whatever materials you apply to it. The visual effect is very subtle, especially when it is viewed in full color on a large screen.

"U"FILM is manufactured by Hudson Photographic Industries, Inc. A complete kit nicely packaged in a sturdy, corrugated box includes a 25-foot roll of "U"FILM, a tabletop guide for accurate placement of frames, three coloring pencils with sharpener, a splicing block, splicing tape, a single-edge razor blade, four plastic filmstrip storage containers with blank stick-on labels, a Teacher's Guide, and a "how to" demonstration filmstrip. The kit is available from your local audiovisual dealer. Since "U"FILM is the most important item in the kit, you may wish to buy only the "film," which can be purchased separately in 25-, 100-, and 1000-foot lengths.

If you would like to use a "U"FILM-type material in larger sheets in an overhead projector, buy a few sheets of textured or frosted acetate from your local art shop. This material has the same basic properties (like the texture on one side) as "U"FILM but comes in 25" × 40" sheets. These sheets can be cut to fit any overhead projector. Everything that can be done with "U"FILM can also be done with the textured acetate. Any overhead projector can be turned into one of those magic machines that transmit "a giant wonderland of projected visual fabrications."

Depending on what you draw and how you sandwich elements together, your nonphotographic transparencies and filmstrips can't help but radiate their bizarre visual splendor in every direction from the point of projection. The limit of your color spectacle is restricted only by the wildest whims of the imagination, and creating such transparency fabrications is a journey that every child is well equipped to make.

Typing titles or sayings directly on film is no problem.

The splicing block is very helpful when using "U"FILM of the clear 35mm film stock.

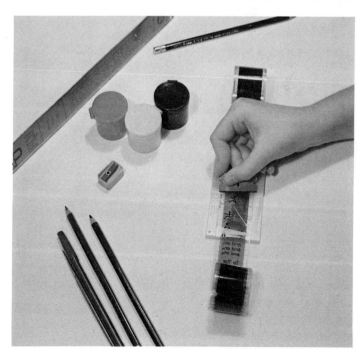

95

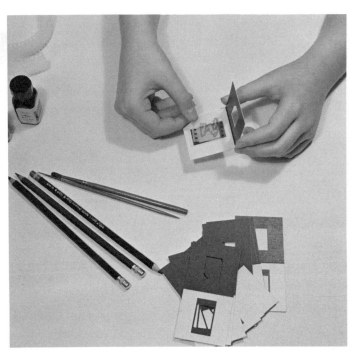

Setting single frames of "U"FILM into cardboard or glass mounts is a nice way to make a slide series.

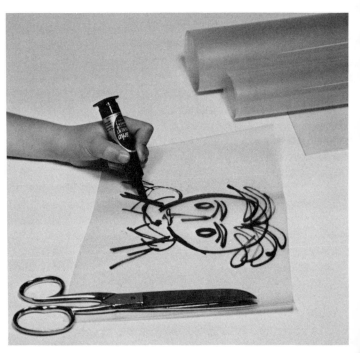

Frosted acetate is very similar to "U"FILM. Draw, paint, type, or what-have-you, and project it on any overhead projector.

Bob can't wait to see his giant designs projected on the screen.

The projected design original is shown here.

Project 20:

Monoprinting

Monoprinting is an art technique that can easily be adapted to photography. In fact, there are several noted photographers who have utilized the technique to create some rather exotic photographs. Calling monoprints photographs, however, is actually a misnomer. There is no camera involved in the making of these images, only some photographic paper, chemicals, and one other magic ingredient.

In "regular" monoprinting, a sheet of glass is used, upon which a design is created directly by painting with a brush, drawing with ink, or what-have-you. Before the design is dry, a sheet of clean paper is placed atop the glass and rubbed gently all over. This helps the paper soak up the wet design. When the paper is removed from the glass, the design has been transferred to the sheet of paper. Hence a print is produced.

This technique is called monoprinting because only **one** print at a time can be made. The glass must be cleaned each time and a new design created before another print can be produced. The inks or paint employed to create the design will usually not yield two prints in a row. Therefore, each print is unique, because its design must first be individually created on the glass.

In adapting this technique to photography, the whole process can be greatly simplified. All you'll need is a jar of petroleum jelly (Vaseline) and your usual photographic paraphernalia. The petroleum jelly, believe it or not, is the "magic" ingredient mentioned earlier! Add some ordinary photographic paper, Dektol, Rapid Fixer, and you're in business.

To see how this technique works, spread some petroleum jelly over the palm and fingers of your left hand. (If you're left-handed, reverse this procedure.) Now with your right hand, press a fresh piece of enlarging paper against your "greased" left hand, and then gently peel the paper away without smearing the jelly.

Of course, you're doing all this under normal room lighting. Usually, photographic paper must be kept away from light, but not in this project. In fact, if you're working in the darkroom, expose the whole sheet to white light for a minute or two, grossly overexposing it after imprinting. Then, place it in a tray of developer for two minutes. Proceed to the stop bath for 30 seconds, and then to the fixer

The materials needed for Project 20 are petroleum jelly, enlarging paper, trays, and chemicals.

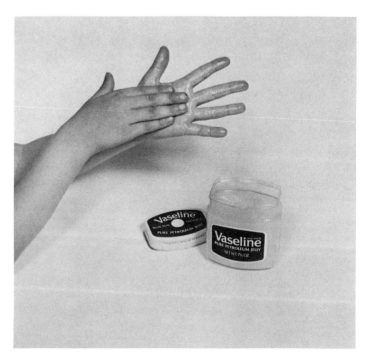

Smear some jelly on your hand.

97

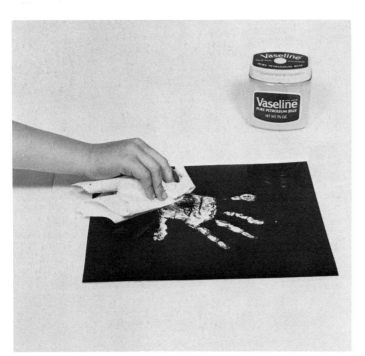

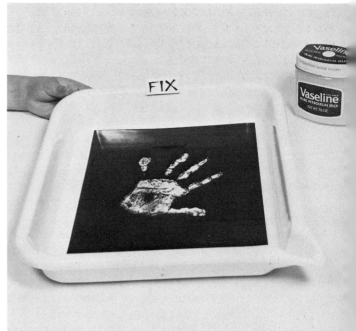

for two minutes. Remove the print from the fixer, wipe off the petroleum jelly, and return it to the fixer for another four minutes. The paper sections that were covered with jelly must also be fixed. Now that you see how the technique works, you can be as creative as you wish—a giant step into "Fantasia Land" is a must.

Obviously, the body parts that can be smeared with petroleum jelly and printed straightaway are many—hands, feet, various sides of the face, ears, elbows, ankles, and even an unsuspecting belly button. Nevertheless, body parts are not the limits of your printing experiences. Anything that can be smeared with a little jelly can be printed. Try leaves, weeds, flowers, string, sponges, or whatever is handy.

An interesting variation of this technique is to use the petroleum jelly as a medium in itself and apply it directly to the paper. You can use a finger-painting approach simply by smearing a little jelly on the paper to create a design. Also, place a little smear of jelly on a plate and try dipping various objects into the jelly and then applying them to the paper in some definite pattern. Use the toy blocks that have letters on them or the ones that have animals or other designs projecting from one face of the block. Use such readily available objects first and then make some printable objects yourself. For example, carve a design on one end of a bar of Ivory soap. Dip it into some petroleum jelly and print it on the paper a number of times to create a basic motif.

As you can see, there's no end to the possibilities inherent in this technique. Kids are particularly ingenious in devising different interpretations. After all, a jar of petroleum jelly can go a long way when it takes only one little smear to do the job.

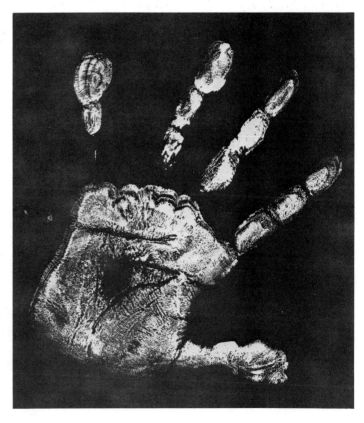

Press a sheet of enlarging paper against the jelly (top, left).

Develop and fix as usual (top, right).

Remove the jelly from the face of print (far left).

Fix for another four minutes (left).

Wash and dry the paper as usual (top, this page).

This is the product of a hand print (near right).

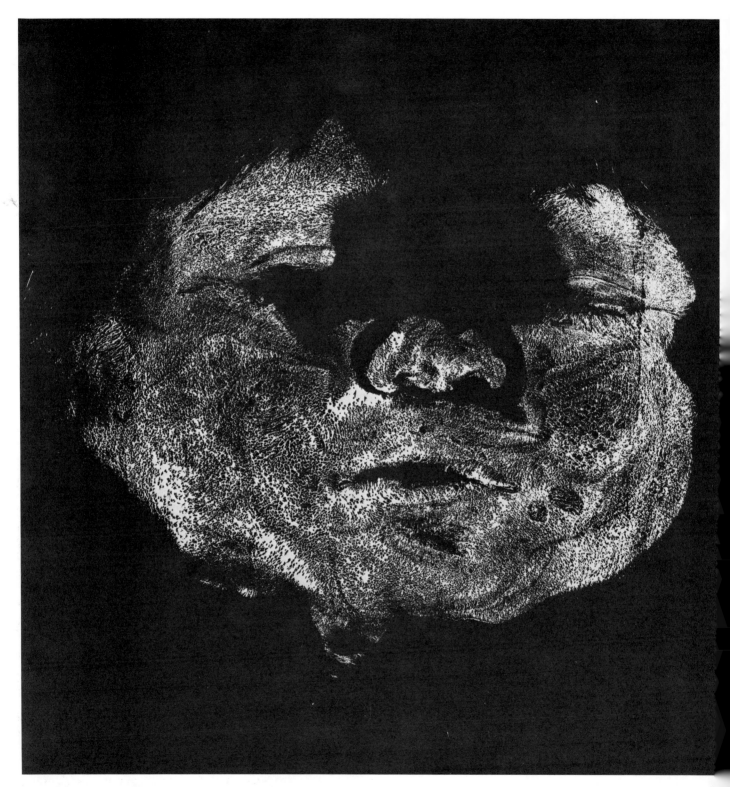

Shown here is a full face view.

Project 21:

The Dream Image

The painter is not alone in his capacity to fabricate a world of his own. The photographer can also produce pictures that depict a very personal reality. Many people, however, still maintain that photography is not an art. They believe that photography is only "a means of reproduction."

Granted, the photographer must always deal with what lies directly in front of the lens. The camera is basically a box with a hole that admits light when you press a button. This light impresses itself on the film in the camera as a latent, or undeveloped, image that is later developed and printed. It is so simple that Eastman Kodak has built a financial empire on the slogan "You press the button and we do the rest." Men, women, and children the world over quickly learn to use the little black box to produce memorabilia galore.

Today, the use of photography in one form or another is still the quickest and easiest way to produce a permanent image of what we see. Records, records, and more records—whether we call them pictures, photos, or snapshots—seem to accumulate in the strangest places. We instinctively gather them as precious mementos of faces and places that are too easily forgotten with the passing of time. Photography has indeed become the bosom buddy of every man in the street. This, of course, does not belittle the medium in any way. Many great photographers are also great recorders, but photography can be used for more than documentation.

Photographers do dream; they fabricate worlds that can appear only through the eyes of the artist. The camera does indeed lend itself to the purposes of imaginative art. In the hands of the artist or the innocent child, the camera is no mere recording device. The photographer, like the painter, can invent and concoct the most unlikely realities. (The child often does it by error.)

If two pictures of the real world are placed one over the other, they can no longer be considered a document. As the two images intermingle, they create the same kind of unreality that is characteristic of a dream. Any image blended with another image causes a certain visual tension. Being unable to readily identify and label this type of imagery, the viewer is forced to decipher its meanings in terms that are more personal than rational.

Multiple exposures can create mystery, intrigue, and myth.

The overlapping of two incongruous scenes can make a rather poignant statement; this one's a graveyard over a highway.

Not too unlike the painter, the photographer can seek to create a world rather than record an event. Multiple imagery is only one of the devices or techniques available to the creative photographer for his own personal expression. The child needs little prodding; he just seems to appropriate the technique quite naturally.

A single image is impressed on the film when you release the shutter button of your camera. But what happens when you forget to advance the film to the next frame and press the button again? Two images are superimposed on the same piece of film. In effect, you have committed an error and have inadvertently made a double exposure. Camera manufacturers have worked very hard to produce cameras that prevent accidental double exposures. Most cameras today have a built-in mechanism that serves this purpose.

Only the most inexpensive cameras will allow you to simply recock the shutter to make another exposure on the same frame. Most cameras will recock the shutter only as the film is advanced to the next frame, thus preventing double exposures. If you use an inexpensive cam-

A picture of a Bruegel painting entitled "Hunters in the Snow" superimposed over a real snowscape makes a fascinating product (top, left).

A piano keyboard and hands exposed three times produces the unique feeling of playing the piano (bottom).

era like the Diana or one of those venerable old cameras like the Argus C-3, you will have no problem making intentional double exposures. In fact, you can make as many exposures as you wish on the same piece of film.

Just remember to give each successive shot on the same frame **one stop less** exposure than that indicated for the normal exposure in the situation. Each separate shot is deliberately underexposed so that the sum exposure of these shots on the frame will equate to the proper exposure for the total frame when you are finished. Then develop and print the negative normally. If there is some overexposure, you can simply use a little more exposure when printing the negative.

The production of some fascinating photographic images is inherent to the technique of multiple exposures. Children are especially facile at producing exotic multiple images. Theirs is the gift of serendipity. They seem to have a natural aptitude for making unusual pictures quite by accident. Like a reverie, their multiple imagery always offers the viewer a fanciful journey into a world that we can all enjoy.

A multiple exposure of various people, some pigeons, and a park synthesizes the essential atmosphere of the park (top, right).

This multiple exposure of a tree, a hydrant, and a lake is interesting (bottom).

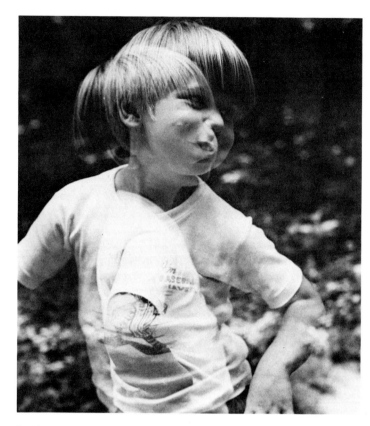

On this page and the next two pages are some more examples of how you and your child can use your imaginations and get some fascinating pictures.

Project 22:

The Game of Repetition

Children learn to see what they are taught to see. In fact, we all see only what we want to see, and what we want to see is usually what we've been taught to see. This little perceptual tidbit can be found in any elementary psychology text.

Simple as it sounds, our seeing is not only **influenced** by what we've been taught, but also **hindered** by what we've been taught. Breaking out of this trap and shattering our "closures" (as our psychologist friends like to call them) is not a simple matter. We can, however, promote techniques that will aid in breaking the limits of our vision. Children are especially open to suggestions for expanding their vision. Fortunately, they do not have to contend with the visual encumbrances of half a lifetime.

There is definitely something quite basic about the nature of the photographic experience that seems to promote better visualization on the part of the person using the camera. Good photography and a person's self-generated level of awareness seem to have much in common. The actual experience of making pictures with a camera has a tremendous impact on a person's general level of perception, if seriously pursued. It seems to cohere various aspects of an individual's perceptual apparatus that heretofore functioned through separate sensory modalities. Photography can be a truly synaesthetic experience. In any case, the cooperative action of several senses as they seek to override their separate functions produces the feeling that a very personal "reality" is somehow being detached and carefully packaged for further consideration by virtue of the act of photographing it.

From time to time, we have all had these moments of heightened awareness where everything just seems to fall into one nice, neat, little package. Children probably enjoy this phenomenon even more than adults do. When it does occur, however, we simply cannot understand how things could ever be any other way. There's a certain feeling of "rightness" about it all. Photography helps to promote this kind of experience. That's why so many of us are addicted to the medium.

We all know that the activities of seeing and look-

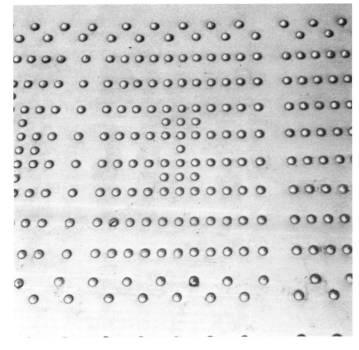

Rivets make a fascinating repetition pattern in the side of a bridge.

The tall grasses shown here look almost like a line drawing.

Here, a display of cracker tins makes an interesting pattern.

The fire wood within the wire fence has an abstract look to it.

ing are not exactly the same thing. Seeing is a natural gift that we acquire soon after birth. We begin to see regardless of the efforts of ourselves or others. Looking, on the other hand, is always a more calculated endeavor. At any age, it's always a matter of directing one's attention to selected aspects of awareness.

Let's consider the nature of attention for a moment. We understand what it means to be attentive, but do we always differentiate between the various aspects of attention that are at our disposal at any given moment? For example, the state of **diffused attention** can certainly prevent us from getting hit by a car while crossing the street, but basically it's a very passive state. Our attention is everywhere at once, yet nowhere specific. With this kind of attention, we can manage to go up and down stairs, open and close doors, and even drive a car. In short, much of our time is taken up by this rather passively receptive state.

If someone were standing on a ledge ten stories up and threatening to jump, the state of **captured attention** would occur. The same is true when we are completely engrossed in a fascinating book, movie, or TV program. In the state of captured attention, our attention is literally seized and riveted to the specifics of the situation. We are, for the most part, prisoners of the occasion.

Directed attention is always deliberate and intentional. We exercise, by choice, a certain self-prescribed measure of control over our attention by intentionally directing it toward a definite goal. Directed attention comes into play whenever we try to do something that is not habitual, like the first few times we try to ice skate, ride a bike, or drive a car. Actually, we have to forcefully direct our attention whenever we want to learn something new.

This state of **directed attention** occurs much more frequently when a person uses a camera. The camera itself makes you much more aware of the fact that you are **looking** at a scene and not just **seeing** it. It is this kind of looking (with the camera helping to direct attention) that can help a person learn to "see." Through photography, you begin to see what is **really** there and not only what you **think** is there.

Learning to "see" with the camera can easily be made into a game—a game that we can play by ourselves or with others wherever and whenever circumstances permit. Since we see our world the way we want to see it, let us see it in a **particular** way. Let us try to purposefully impose one specific "closure" on our own way of seeing so as to temporarily nullify or inhibit other closures that serve only to restrict and limit our vision.

For example, one game could be called "The Repetition Game." The main task in this game is to look for and see only the visual **similarities** in our world. This means that we must explore and examine our visual world in terms of the repetition of similar shapes that occur in our environment. A rhythm-in-seeing will readily unfold through the practice and development of this kind of visual alliteration. By imposing such visual limitations on ourselves, we can consciously use our powers of concentration and directed attention to promote visual configurations that would not normally exist. We can rise above our usual visual limitations by resorting to short but concerted efforts to see in other ways.

The improvements achieved through such periods of directed attention may be short lived, but our relative achievements become easier to maintain through practice, and such practice makes for new and better habits of seeing. In several of the upcoming projects, we shall examine more visual games that can be presented to children to help them delimit and expand their vision. Try making up your own variations of these visual games as you go along. Or, you might use the suggestions mentioned here as a springboard to creating a whole new series of visual gymnastics that kids will just love to explore.

The concrete shapes (above) form a dark, curving pattern evoking a somber mood. The next three pages have some other imaginative examples of repetitive images.

Project 23:

The Game of Signs

Expanding our awareness by learning to see and appreciate aspects of our surroundings that generally pass us by demands a certain amount of visual concentration. In order to become aware of the various features of our surroundings to which we are generally oblivious, we have to learn to control the ideas that impede and restrict perception. If we want to develop and increase our sensitivity to the point where we can actually enjoy the full flavor of our surroundings, we must learn to explore and examine that environment in purely **visual** terms.

In our discussion of "closure" in the last project, we began to see how we could utilize purposeful closure to nullify, or at least suppress, habits that limit our increased visual awareness. In other words, we tried to promote a specific manner of visualization to which we do not generally subscribe, while at the same time minimizing the "normal" limitations on our seeing.

For example, by emphasizing a more visual attitude, a pile of tires is not seen as **just** a pile of tires, but is actually perceived as a fascinating repetition of circles. A trite illustration? Maybe. But try it; it works. It is simply the change in attitude that makes the difference in our seeing. Even a suggestion of change has a considerable impact on seeing.

In "The Game of Signs," we are going to seek out and explore various kinds of signs, but we will disregard any possible verbal meanings in order to tap the resources of their visual content. By avoiding the verbal message and trying to become more sensitive to the inherent visual qualities that these signs can afford us, we can actually develop a broader range of visual awareness.

The signs that we should look for can be anything from a large, weathered billboard-size poster to insignificant graffiti in the center of an otherwise commonplace door. The important thing to remember is that an intensification of vision demands that we look at the world around us with increased concentration. This can be achieved more easily by using some device for visual isolation, like a piece of poster board with a rectangle cut out of it, or better still, the viewfinder of your camera.

The growth of one aspect of our awareness sometimes necessitates the short-circuiting of another avenue of our perception. While we seek out visually interesting

This is a shot of a deteriorated billboard poster on the side of a building.

A poster advertising clean clothes is shown in the front window of dry cleaning store.

aspects of our environment, we should keep in abeyance our insistence on assigning meanings and verbal significance to what we see. Since signs, in whatever form they may take, can also perform as cryptic images with visual implications quite apart from the verbal message intended, we should try to use them only as starting points for our adventures in visual exploration.

First of all, regardless of the verbal message, signs can be explored and appreciated for their own sake. Only by eliminating the obvious message can we begin to really appreciate the possible visual import that signs may hold as images in their own right. Secondly, by allowing signs to suggest meanings different from the intended verbal message, we can begin to understand the restrictive effects that much of our learning has on the growth and expansion of our visual awareness.

We do indeed sacrifice a great deal in the name of "education." Learning to "see" does not negate any of the more verbal aspects of the school curriculum. Reading and writing are still fundamental to everyone's education. However, we should begin to admit to ourselves that an acceptance of the validity of certain nonverbal approaches to knowledge is long overdue. Why must we limit ourselves to educating only part of the person? A medium like photography can open new aspects of learning and disclose novel modes of understanding.

Here are some more signs taken in different places, such as brick wall (above); a beach, where a love sign scrawled in the sand was about to be washed away (below, left); and a street, where snow covered part of the direction signs (below, right).

Project 24:

The Figure/Ground Game

Most of us are familiar with the basic figure/ground concepts of Gestalt psychology. For example, as we look around the room, the things we see tend to become isolated from their backgrounds. Looking at the picture on the wall, we see only the picture, not the wall. Shifting our eyes to a book on the table, we see only the book, not the table. There is no **physical** reason why objects should stand out from their backgrounds, but they do. Any basic psychology book will tell us that this visual peculiarity is a feature of the nervous system.

Since the figure/ground phenomenon is a normal occurrence in our vision, let's make a game out of controlling and varying this visual experience. To begin with, take an object, any object; stare at it for a few moments and notice how its shape becomes more and more precise. Try to grasp its exact shape and nothing else. At first your attention is likely to wander, but with a little effort you can maintain your concentration. As you gaze at the object, define its surroundings. Draw an imaginary fence around the object. Suddenly you will find that the object takes on a certain visual excitement all its own. It is as if you have never really seen the object before. You will notice qualities and properties that you didn't know existed.

Now direct your gaze **behind** the object. Notice how the background leaps out at you. Instead of looking at the object, look at the **spaces around** the object. These spaces take on a new importance, a new meaning. This is what the artist calls negative form.

Try alternating visually between the object and its background. Shift your gaze back and forth between the figure and the background. Notice how perception of both the figure and the background increases your awareness of the whole. A definite unity occurs between the object and its background. With a certain amount of concerted effort on your part, the full integration of the object with its background willl manifest itself. The whole becomes more than its parts. For a moment, the object and its background seem inseparable; a kind of completeness takes place, something that we seldom can experience during the onrush of daily life.

To experiment further with figure/ground relationships, consider a rather large object, like a tree. Separate

A shadow on a wooden boardwalk provides stark contrasts.

Wheel spokes, some in sharp focus, some in soft focus, make an intriguing abstract picture.

The shadow of sticks on sand produces a man on the cross symbol (top).

White statuary stands in bold relief against a dark background (bottom).

the tree from its background; then separate the background from the tree. As you begin to weld the figure and its background together, walk around the tree slowly and watch how your perspective changes. Notice how the tree and its background change in relation to each other. The sudden awareness of how still objects move in relation to each other as we ourselves move in relation to those objects can be a delightful visual experience.

As a variant on the figure/ground game, let's examine how we would handle something a little more symbolic, like shadows. Imagine a world where shadows are more real than the objects that cast them. Absurd? Yes, but still a good exercise in the kind of imagination necessary to separate a form from its background. Such an implausible possibility can provide us with a visual journey into a make-believe world that needs no invention, but simply requires a slight shift in our customary patterns of awareness—not a difficult task.

On any bright, sunny day, everyone and everything will cast a shadow. Since shadows are everywhere, start first by selecting and observing a specific configuration. View the shadow that the form creates as inseparable from the form itself. Seek to visualize the shadow or silhouette first as an inseparable companion to the mother form, and then slowly allow the shadow to take on more and more visual importance until it assumes complete prominence in the scene.

In the picture of the pigeons, the shadow created by the bird in the center of the composition easily predominates. The shadow of the bird provides a greater visual impact than the pigeon itself. The importance of the bird is definitely reduced as we concentrate more and more on its shadow.

By shifting our awareness to shadows as the principal subject for a composition, we begin a process of abstraction that seeks to perceive reality more in terms of visually interesting formations. The eyes then begin to serve a purpose that goes far beyond the more mundane matters of navigating up or down stairs and across streets.

Shadows do make fascinating visual configurations. Isolated from the mother form, a shadow can have its own reality. Observe shadows either with a camera or with just a large rectangle cut out of a piece of mat board. See how easily a shadow can be instilled with a personality of its own just by the way in which you see it. Notice how it presents a life of its own—a life that is full of potentialities for the photographer's eye.

The success of anyone's journey into the land of shadows is limited only by the extent of that individual's imagination. Shadows can be charged with a dynamism all their own, but they become meaningful only if we are willing to relax our perceptual fixation on the objects that cast them in order to play the figure/ground game.

Here, two people are standing near a window in a church (top).

Firemen putting out a fire in a cloud of smoke gives this photo an eerie quality (bottom).

117

A girl's shadow on a boat next to the water produces an ''other worldly'' figure (top).

The shadow of the trees is complemented by the many tiny weeds that are dispersed across the surface of the relatively unobtrusive snow (bottom).

Project 25:

A Quixotic Vision

Look out on a new world by simply changing your visual orientation. Strange things can happen when you radically shift your point of view. The whole world seems to become suddenly inhabited by exotic forms. Looking at the world from an unconventional position is foreign to most of us, but just imagine how uniquely different our environment would appear from a worm's-eye or bird's-eye view.

Trying to look at our world from a worm's-eye view is not easy, especially since our eyes are not located near our feet. Viewing the world from the ground up can be easily simulated, however, by using any good-size mirror and placing it on the floor or ground beside whatever subject matter we intend to survey. In photography, the child can easily place his camera in a very low position to achieve this same worm's-eye view. Seeing and photographing the world around us from the ground up can provide some very startling results.

Similarly, viewing our world from an extremely high vantage point can shed a new light on the nature of our environment. By placing the same mirror at arm's length above our heads, we can look directly down on most of our everyday environment and again radically shift our point of view. By taking pictures from a second- or third-story window or from a bridge or balcony, or even by simply pointing the camera directly down to the sidewalk, we can sometimes jar our perceptual complacency just enough to produce fascinating and often bizarre visual configurations.

Though modern psychology tells us that we tend to react to our world as we perceive it, the radical shifting of our point of view to a worm's-eye or bird's-eye position for short periods of time will not drastically alter our attitudes. It can afford us a quixotic break from the monotony of seeing the world we live in as we usually do.

Children are especially fascinated with unusual perceptual frames of reference. The worm's-eye and bird's-eye viewing positions can provide interesting variations in the way images are visually put together. The oddities in perspective that occur as a result of these extreme angles of view help to dispel many preconceived notions as to just what is "good" or "bad" pictorial composition.

Here's an air conditioning fixture on a ceiling.

This is a shot of a determined child climbing up a slide.

119

Seeing the world with a fresh eye is frequently the result of viewing the world in an unconventional manner. We spend far too much time shackled to a single point of view. A radical departure from our usual eye-level viewing position can provide unique insights into the limitations of normal perception.

As we have already mentioned, seeing and looking are not quite the same thing; there is a difference. We are all born with the capacity to see, but each of us must **learn to look.** Normal seeing is a rather passive and receptive mode of perception, while looking is very much an active, creative, and participatory venture. Most of the time we simply see. Only after we have learned to look, or at least learned to **try** to look, do we sometimes begin to see. This kind of seeing is obviously very precious. Children have a natural inclination and facility for the kind of look-

This shot is of a girl talking on the telephone (left).

Here's a shot of some open windows on the side of a building (bottom).

120

ing that leads to seeing. This is why great care must be taken not to quash them in their formative years.

Photography can be very helpful in nurturing the child's vision. Since the camera helps to distance the observer from the subject, the child can be better prepared to really **look** at it and perceive it as it is, not as he **thinks** it is. Hence, the development of a new kind of vision, one in which seeing is a creative act of participation on the part of the viewer, not just a record-making procedure. This is why teaching photography to kids is such fun. For the most part, they can photograph their world quite directly without feeling foolish about the results. They don't have to prove anything. They accept what they see through the viewfinder of the camera, and they approve of the product—the picture. After all, that's what was there, wasn't it? It's all so simple!

Here's a bird's-eye view of three people at a telephone booth (right).

Here's a shot looking up at the trees as they converge in the sky (bottom).

This is a toe-level view of working man.

Sources and Resources

Teaching photography to kids can be exciting and rewarding. A few enthusiastic youngsters, a little money, and some basic "how-to" information are all that's required. Knowing how kids are attracted to the medium, and assuming you can manage to get the funds, where do you begin to look for the kind of information you'll need to turn those kids on to photography?

As you'll see from the assortment of materials outlined here, much of it is basic information that must be tailored to meet the needs of the prescribed situation. Since photography in the schools is still in its infancy, anyone who decides to take the initiative must learn to pick and choose from a relatively wide range of materials and be able to shape them to fit his or her own particular circumstance. The reference information that follows is an overview of possible sources and resources that may prove helpful in providing children with photography and photography-related experiences. Under the heading Products, you will find all the materials needed for the projects outlined in the text arranged in alphabetical order. Included are the companies that manufacture or distribute the materials and their addresses.

This list of sources and resources is by no means meant to be exhaustive. However, it does provide a sampling of some of the materials presently available for teaching photography to children. Much still has to be done with photography in the schools. Only recently have we become aware that our precious verbalization process may not be our primary mode of thinking! In fact, many contemporary psychologists and philosophers are beginning to postulate that maybe the mind does not really think primarily in words after all, but rather in images. If this proves to be true, then for more generations than we care to count, we may be guilty of having educated only half the child, and leaving the other half practically untouched. Photography may not be our panacea, but it is an important tool in helping to provide every child with a more balanced approach to education.

Audiovisual Aids

AV-COM, Inc.. Educational Media Division, 4019 Westerly Place, Suite 111, Newport Beach, Calif. 92660. Prices vary with product ($12.50 to $22.50). Produces slide/script demonstrator kits that cover the basics—developing film, enlarging, processing prints, and even dry mounting. Each process is covered with between 10 to 20 2" × 2" slides, keyed in visually to a step-by-step printed text.

Camera Series, Creative Photography, Darkroom Series, Film Loading Series. Media Research and Development, Arizona State University, Tempe, Ariz. 85281. Except for the **Film Loading Series** (three films and cassettes), which costs $40, each series costs $120. (Individual parts of the filmstrip series are available for $22.50 each.) Should be used in the upper grades. Each program is handsomely packaged in storage albums; however, the actual filmstrip frames should be mounted in individual half-frame mounts for better durability.

Fine Photographic Slide Sets. Light Impressions Corp., P.O. Box 3012, Rochester, N.Y. 14614. Price varies with each program. Written material on each artist plus slides.

Getting Into Photography. Training Information Center, Gilbert Altschul Productions, Inc., Chicago, Ill. 60614. $95. Comes with a printed script and teacher's guide containing questions and answers, suggested follow-up activities, and assignments.

Images of Man, I & II. Scholastic Book Services, 904 Sylvan Ave., Englewood Cliffs, N.J. 07632. Each program, including slides, cassette, and teaching guide, is $175. Conceived and designed by Cornell Capa of the International Center for Photography in New York City, this is one of the best audiovisual programs to hit the market in recent years. An assemblage of photo essays by some of the world's great photographers, with the artists themselves talking about their work.

Kodak Materials for Visual-Communication Education and Training, ED-2-1. Eastman Kodak Company, Photo Information, Dept. 454, 343 State Street, Rochester, N.Y. 14650. Replete with instructional materials at reasonable cost.

Photography: A History. Educational Dimensions Corp., Box 126, Stamford, Conn. 06904. Cassette version $49.50. A good introduction to the entire history of photography, this two-part color/sound filmstrip stresses the development of the medium as an art.

Photography: A Special Way of Seeing. GAF Corp., Photo Education Service, 140 W. 51st St., New York, N.Y. 10020. Write (on your school letterhead) for a free loan print. For beginning photo classes on the secondary school level, the film is based on a collection of outstanding color slides and black-and-white prints that emphasize the personal, creative approach to photography. Essentially motivational rather than instructional.

So You Don't Have Any Ideas? ENCORE, Inc., 1235 South Victory Blvd., Burbank, Calif. 91502. Cassette version $49. A color/sound filmstrip set to spark up an already established photo program. It is broken down into four parts: "Take Another Look," "What's Your Angle," "Look at the Ordinary Thing," and "Look—Where You Live."

Your Programs From Kodak, AT-1. Eastman Kodak Company, Photo Information, Dept. 841, 343 State St., Rochester, N.Y. 14650. Catalog full of various teaching aids for photography. Lists numerous film and slide programs available free on loan to schools and other institutions.

Books

Burke, Tom. **Do It In The Dark.** P.O. Box 5367 Tucson, Ariz. 85703; H. P. Books, 1975. $5.95. A very concise and graphic darkroom manual that even includes a chapter on color printing. A book that's easy for kids to get into and stay with.

Classroom Projects Using Photography; Part I—For the Elementary School Level, Part II—For the Secondary School Level. Rochester, N.Y. 14650: Eastman Kodak Company. $6.95 each. Both good as reference materials that generate ideas which can be blended into everyday classroom activities.

Cooke, Robert W. **Designing With Light.** 50 Portland St., Worcester, Mass. 01608: Davis Publications, Inc., 1969. $5.95. Introduces the photographic medium through cameraless photography. Includes materials and techniques, basic visual guidelines and historical perspective.

Czaja, Paul Clement. **Writing With Light: A Simple Workshop in Basic Photography.** 15 Wilmot Lane, Riverside, Conn. 06878: The Chatham Press, Inc., 1973. $5.95. An interesting approach to photography with children.

Elam, Jane. **Photography, Simple and Creative.** 450 W. 33rd St., New York, N.Y. 10001: Van Nostrand Reinhold Co., 1975. $5.95. Present creative projects that the more advanced photo students might like to pursue.

Fineman, Mark. **The Home Darkroom.** 750 Zeckendorf Blvd., Garden City, N.Y. 11530: Amphoto, Second Edition, 1976. $3.95. How to set up your own darkroom with step-by-step instructions on darkroom procedures.

Fransecky, Roger B. and John Debes. **Visual Literacy: A Way to Learn—A Way to Teach.** Publications Dept., 1201 16th St., N.W. Washington, D.C. 20036: Association for Educational Communications and Technology. An introduction to visual literacy as a part of photographic education. The AECT also has a whole series of audiovisual materials relating to visual literacy. (They may be obtained from the aforementioned address.)

Hertzberg, Robert. **Elementary Developing and Printing.** 750 Zeckendorf Blvd., Garden City, N.Y. 11530 Amphoto, Second Revised Printing 1977. $8.95. Offers good pointers on how to improvise darkroom facilities (This publisher offers a wealth of basic "how to" books. Write for the catalog.)

Holland, Viki. **How To Photograph Your World.** 597 Fifth Ave., New York, N.Y. 10017: Charles Scribner's Sons, 1974. $5.95. A simple, basic approach to photography for kids.

Holter, Patra. **Photography Without A Camera.** 450 W. 33rd St., New York, N.Y. 10001: Van Nostrand Reinhold Co., 1972. $8.95. Presents a camera-less photography project to introduce the medium to practically any age group. Includes techniques and materials, visual guidelines, and historical perspective.

Jacobs, Mark and Ken Kokrda. **Photography In Focus.** 750 Zeckendorf Blvd., Garden City, N.Y. 11530: Amphoto. $6.95. Written by experienced teachers who have taught at all levels. Explains the entire photographic process in an easy-to-understand, step-by-step manner and is reinforced with numerous photographs, drawings, and charts.

Curriculum Guide For Photography. 8259 Niles Center Rd., Skokie, III. 60076: National Textbook Company. $2. A 98-page guide to setting up a photography course, including chapter-by-chapter curriculum outlines. Complements the aforementioned **Photography In Focus.**

Jacobson, R. E. **Photoguide to Home Processing.** 750 Zeckendorf Blvd., Garden City, N.Y. 11530: Amphoto, 1973. $5.95. The darkroom at home. How to set it up and the processing steps that can be accomplished.

Karsten, Kenneth S. **Abstract Photography Techniques.** 750 Zeckendorf Blvd., Garden City, N.Y. 11530: Amphoto, 1970. $14.50. Abstract photo techniques through creative projects.

Meiselas, Susan. **Learn to See.** P101, Polaroid Corp., 549 Technology Sq., Cambridge, Mass. 02139: Polaroid Foundation. $3. A source book of ideas in photography for the classroom situation.

Muse, Ken. **PHOTO ONE: Basic Photo Text.** Englewood Cliffs, N.J. 07632: Prentice-Hall, Inc., 1973. $6.95. A text that presents a very amusing way of getting basic information across to the upper-grade student.

Peter and His Camera. 145 Palisade St., Dobbs Ferry, N.Y. 10522: Morgan & Morgan, 1973. $2.95. Parents of young children may be interested in this book, written in narrative form and illustrated in full color. Covers most of the basics of photography in a straightforward, easy-to-understand manner. Especially well suited for experiences with cartridge-loading cameras. Teachers of the early grades may use the book in conjunction with the Snapshooter project.

Schrank, Jeffrey. **Understanding Media.** 8259 Niles Center Rd., Skokie, III. 60076: National Textbook Company, 1975. $7.45. A good foundation for relating photography to media in general.

Shipman, Carl. **Understanding Photography.** P.O. Box 5367, Tucson, Ariz. 85703: H. P. Books, 1974. $5.95. Covers the theory of photography, including some very sophisticated material. However, easy to read and understand.

Shull, Jim. **The Hole Thing: A Manual of Pinhole Fotografy.** 145 Palisade St., Dobbs Ferry, N.Y. 10522: Morgan & Morgan, 1974. $2.95. An excellent primer on pinhole photography.

Suid, Murray. **Painting with the Sun: A First Book of Photography.** 60 Commercial Wharf, Boston, Mass. 02110: Dynamic Learning Corp., 1973. $2.95. For the teacher in the grade school. Comes with a teacher's manual that shows how photography can be related to the general school program, including such disciplines as language arts, science, social studies, math, and art. Includes an overview of possible operating costs.

Webster, David. **Photo Fun, An Idea Book for Shutter Bugs.** 845 Third Ave., New York, N.Y. 10022: Franklin Watts, Inc., 1973. $4.95. Illustrates with detailed drawings how many of the more popular photo tricks are accomplished.

Other Publications

Camera Cookbook, The. Workshop For Learning Things, Inc., 5 Bridge St., Watertown, Mass. 02172. $1.25. Designed much like a recipe book, this publication outlines in detail a step-by-step approach to photography based on the use of the Diana camera.

Click and Print. Workshop For Learning Things, Inc., 5 Bridge St., Watertown, Mass. 02172. $1.25. A "how to" effort by sixth graders in a nearby school in which the writing, photographs, drawings, book design, and layout were done entirely by the kids themselves.

Media Mix: Ideas and Resources on Media and Communications. Claretian Publications, 221 W. Madison St., Chicago, III. 60606. One-year subscription $9. Edited by Jeffrey Schrank, this newsletter covers new films, video, media books, photography, and other items of value to people into media of any kind.

Visual Literacy Newsletter. The Center for Visual Literacy, Taylor Hall, University of Rochester, Rochester, N.Y. 14627. The principal organ of communication for the visual literacy movement. Write for a copy and a membership application.

Products

Aluminum foil. Heavy-duty kind, 200 sq. ft. roll; or aluminum frozen dinner trays or pie pans.

Argus C-3 camera. Sometimes available at the resale camera dept. of your local photo store. Ask your dealer what other camera might facilitate double exposure.

Cartridge-loading cameras, 110. Kodak Trimlite Instamatic 18; Kodak Tele-Instamatic 608; Vivitar 402; Prinz 202; Haminex 100. Local discount stores sometimes have good sales on cartridge-loading cameras.

Cartridge-loading cameras, 126. Kodak X-15F, Kodak X-35F. The newer 126 cameras have the Flipflash bar rather than the former cube-type flash. GAF makes 126 cartridge-loading cameras that are competitively priced. Their model designations change frequently, so check with your local photo dealer. The following company sells an inexpensive line of Instamatic-type cameras; write directly for prices to: Imperial Camera Corp., 421 North Western Avenue, Chicago, Ill. 60612.

Changing bag. Comes in various sizes from 16" × 17" to 27" × 30" under different brand names such as Aplex, Bogen, Capro, etc.

Con-Tact, clear. Sold by the running yard (18" wide). One yard yields: 8 8" × 10" pieces; 15 5" × 7" pieces; 162 2" × 2" pieces. Available in most hardware stores.

Coloring agents (commercial). Commercial toners like Kodak's Blue and Brown Toners; GAF's liquid Flemish, Sepia, and Vivitoner; and Edwal's multicolored sets; etc., are available from your local photo dealer. Edwal, Kodak, and Marshall make photo tint colors in a variety of hues. Write Marshall's for the most extensive listing of coloring agents available at: John G. Marshall Mfg. Co. Inc., 167 N. 9th St., Brooklyn, N.Y. 11211.

Coloring products (household). Cranberry and grape juice, coffee, all-purpose dyes, etc. are all available at local supermarkets.

Darkroom trays (5" × 7" and 8" × 10" sizes). Kodak Duraflex; Yankee developing trays (sets of 3); Peterson print trays (tripak); C V Products, Inc. developing trays (sets of 3), also available in 4" × 6" size; Bogen Hi-Impact photo trays.

Developing bath. Developers come in powder or liquid form, in pints, quarts, and gallons. For use with a group of children, it is better to buy the gallon-size powder form. Mix in a plastic pail with a plastic spoon and store in brown glass bottles. The developers are available from local photo stores under various brand names: Edwal, Ethol, FR, GAF, Kodak, etc.

Diana camera. When buying less than a dozen cameras at a time, use the following distributors: Workshop For Learning Things, Inc., 5 Bridge Street, Watertown, Mass. 02172; Sax Arts and Crafts, 207 North Milwaukee Street, Milwaukee, Wis. 53202 ($1.60 each plus shipping). Cameras will usually cost more than $1 when purchased in small quantities. For the best price, buy the case (72 cameras at 99¢ each plus shipping) directly from the wholesaler: Power Sales Co., Box 113, Willow Grove, Pa. 19090. Film may also be purchased at a discount from the above suppliers. Compare prices with local photo store. Sometimes outdated film is available cheaply from local sources or army surplus outlets. Check Yellow Pages or ask your local dealer. Remember that the Diana uses only the 120/220 size film.

Drawing and painting supplies. Waterproof felt markers; crayons; acrylic paints; tempera and watercolor paints; colored inks; pastels; colored acetates; transfer letters; finger paints; block printing ink. Available from your local art supply store.

Dry mounting tissue. Kodak Dry Mounting Tissue, Type 2; Seal Color Mount Tissue; Technal Dry Mounting Tissue. All available in sizes: 4" × 5" to 16" × 20" (8" × 10" is recommended).

Easels. Speed-Ez-Els, size: 2½" × 3½", 3½" × 5", 4" × 5", 5" × 7", 8" × 10"; Capro adjustable enlarging easel; Premier multiprint easel; Paterson enlarging easel.

Enlargers. C V Developing and Enlarging Kit No. 1111, C V Products, Inc., 5026 27th Ave., Rockford, Ill. 61101. Other small enlargers suitable for children include the following: Durst F-30; Paterson 35; Prinz 35; Omega B600; Bogen T35; Vivitar E33.

Enlarging timers. Gra-Lab 300; Mark-Time Photo-Time Switch; Time-O-Lite Darkroom Timer, Model P.

Film clips. Stainless steel bulldog clamps available from local stationery store. Spring-type clothespins can also be used.

Fixing bath. Fixer and rapid fixer, powder or liquid, in pints, quarts, and gallons (reusable). Available in photo stores under a variety of brand names: Kodak; GAF; Edwal; and FR.

Funnel and graduate (16 oz. size). Plastic funnels and graduates of the unbreakable variety are best used with children; Kodak brand is recommended.

Glass (sheet). 5" × 7" or 8" × 10" size is available from local glazier; or 4" × 4" size can be cut for you. Ordinary window glass may be used, but the extra weight of plate glass is recommended. Remember to have the four edges of the glass swiped to prevent cuts on small hands. Prices vary with quantity ordered. A fabricated hinged glass carrier can be cut to fit your enlarger (two pieces of glass taped on one side). Film Proofers and print frames can also be used. Premier Print Frame comes in both 5" × 7" and 8" × 10" sizes and is sturdy, serviceable, and inexpensive.

Glue. Elmer's Glue-All, Duco Cement. Available at local hardware store. Be sure to avoid any kind of spray adhesive. They contain some very harmful ingredients! If you desire adhesive permanence beyond what the aforementioned items can provide, check your local hardware store to see what brands of epoxy cement are available.

Instafilm. Available from: Metro/Kalvar Inc., 745 Post Road, Darien, Conn. 06820. It may also be available from your local AV dealer; check the Yellow Pages.

Instant slide kit. Available from Starex, Inc., 655 Schuler Ave., Kearny, N.J. 07032 and Edmund Scientific Co. Edscorp Building, Barrington, N.J. 08007.

Lamp (with 6" reflector). Use a 25-watt bulb in a 6" spun-aluminum reflector. Available from local hardware or photo store.

Light source. Any enlarger or an ordinary light bulb (approximately 60 to 100 watts) may be used as a light source. A clamp-on light unit can be made with any inexpensive spun-aluminum reflector unit with a 60-watt bulb. Available at your local hardware or discount store.

Lure pocket camera. American Mos, P.O. Box 96, Malverne, N.Y. 11565. $4.99 plus 40¢ postage for camera, color negative film, instructions, and processing. Be sure to return both camera and film for processing. Camera accepts flash.

Mat board. Check your local art supply store to see what brands are available. Ordinary clipboard (similar to mat board but without facing) is cheaper and just as useful for this project, as long as archival stability of image is not warranted.

Paint. Black spray paint (matte finish) in 8, 12, and 16 oz. cans. With very young children, where an aerosol-type spray paint is not practical, any available black tempera paint may be used as a substitute. Available in hardware and discount stores. Tempera paint may have to be purchased in an art supply store. The spray cans are probably available at local discount and hardware stores.

Paper. Ilfospeed, Kodak RC, and Unicolor papers are available in 25, 100, 250, and 500 sheet packages. Resin-coated papers are recommended for use with children because of their much shorter wash and dry times. However, each brand should be tested individually for the proper exposure time. Papers are also manufactured in contrast grades from 1 to 5. For sunny days use grades 2 or 3; on cloudy days use grades 4 or 5. **Photo-enlarging paper:** Kodak RC (normal); Ilfospeed (No. 2 or 3); Unicolor (No. 2 or 3); Luminos (No. 2 or 3). **High-contrast papers:** Kodak RC (extra hard); Ilfospeed (No. 5); Unicolor (No. 5); Agfa (No. 6). Agfa makes the highest contrast paper available, but it is not resin coated. Wash and dry times are much longer; product is archival. **Pastel, metallic, and fluorescent papers:** Luminos Photo Corp., 25 Wolfe St., Yonkers, N.Y. 10705; Spiratone Inc., 135-06 Northern Blvd., Flushing, N.Y. 11354; Delta Import /Distribution, 319 West Erie St., Chicago, Ill. 60610. **P.O.P.:** see Printing-out paper.

Petroleum jelly. Available from your local supermarket or drug store.

Photoenlarging kit. C V Developing and Enlarging Kit (No. 1111), C V Products, Inc., 5026 27th Ave., Rockford, Ill. 61109, $31.95.

Poster board. For the construction of suitable shutter or "barn door," use black poster board or heavy construction paper; comes in various sizes. Available in art supply stores.

Print tongs. Bamboo type recommended (various brand names). Set of two, color coded.

Printing device. An 8" × 10" piece of plate glass. Available from local glazier. Be sure to have edges swiped to prevent cuts on little hands.

Printing frames. Premier Print Frame (highly recommended on the basis of economical cost and suitability for project); Paterson Contact Proof Printer; HPI Film Proofer; Technal Proof Printer. All available from your local photo dealer. **Glass printing frame:** Kodak 3¼" × 4" projector slide cover glass (24 sheets per box). Local glazier can custom-cut 4" × 4" pieces of ordinary window glass. Price varies with quantity.

Printing-out paper (P.O.P.). Kodak Studio Proof F, single weight, sizes 4" × 5", 5" × 7", and 8" × 10" in packages of 25, 100, and 500 sheets. Available at your local photo dealer, or, contact: Consumer Markets Division, Eastman Kodak Co., 345 State St., Rochester, N.Y. 14650. Parallel product marketed by GAF Corp., 140 W. 51st St., New York, N.Y. 10020 and Agfa-Gevaert, Inc., 275 North St., Teterboro, N.J. 07608.

Print-processing drums (daylight). Unidrum II color-print processor; Beseler color-processing drum; Chromega color-print processor. All are available in the following sizes: 8" × 10", 11" × 14", and 16" × 20".

Quick-slide kits. Come in 20-slide and 75-slide sizes. Available from: Edmund Scientific Co., Edscorp Building, Barrington, N.J. 08007; or Quick-Slide, Box 517, Dept. A, Englishtown, N.J. 07726.

Safelight. Any red bulb of low wattage will do if there is a light fixture in the darkroom. A very practical substitute is an ordinary flashlight with several layers of red gelatin over the light. A Boy Scout-type flashlight is handy to have, because it has a flat end that facilitates standing it upright and a right-angle light source that directs the light to where it is needed. Use heavy-duty energy cells for greater light life. Available at most hardware or discount stores.

Slide kit (60-second). Starex, Inc., 655 Schuler Ave., Kearny, N.J. 07032.

Slide mounts. Kodak 2" × 2" Slide Cover Glass; Kodak Metal Binders (for above); GEPE 2" × 2" Precision Slide Binders; EMDE 2" × 2" Slide Glass; Kinderman 2" × 2" Slide Binders; Kodak 3¼" × 4" Projector Slide Cover Glass; EMDE 3¼" × 4" Slide Glass. Kodak 2" × 2" Slide Cover Glass provides a quick, inexpensive method of glass-mounting slides. Note: Edges must be taped to fasten slide together. Snap-together glass mounts are also sold under a number of brand names: Gepe, Brumberger, Emde, Esco, Kinderman, Lindia, Star-D, Titania. Be sure to consider thickness of the assembled mount in relation to the specific projector to be used. Local glazier can cut 2" × 2" squares from 1/16" Plexiglas, if plastic is preferable for little fingers. Cost varies.

Snapshooter camera. When buying less than a dozen cameras at a time, use the following distributor: Visual Motivations Co., Division of KFL, Regal Road, King of Prussia, Pa. 19406 ($2 each with either black-and-white or color film). For quantity purchases, buy directly from the manufacturer: Plastic Development Corporation, 9810 Ashton Road, Philadelphia, Pa. 19114. The Snapshooter is sold with film; replacement cartridges (126-size) available from local photo dealer. For limited quantity purchases, some art suppliers or craft shops sometimes stock a similar item. For example, try: Sax Arts and Crafts, 207 North Milwaukee St., Milwaukee, Wis. 53202.

Stirring paddle (or plastic spoon). Kodak stirring paddle sold individually, 10" long.

Sunlamp. Ordinary sunlight is the preferred light source. However, a sunlamp can be used **with extreme caution.** Children should **never** look at the bulb. Allow bulb to warm up for 5 minutes before using. A 275-watt Sylvania or GE sunlamp with a 6″ reflector that completely covers the lamp can be fixed to the edge of a table facing the floor (so it is below eye level). Available in most department stores and some hardware stores.

Tanks. Daylight film processing tank: Kodacraft roll-film tank, two aprons for 135mm or one apron for 120mm film; GAF developing tank and reel (plastic and adjustable film size); Yankee-Clipper II roll-film tank (similar to aforementioned); Jobo developing tank (with adjustable reel); Paterson tank (with adjustable reel); FR "special" roll-film developing tank. **Roll-film tank:** The simplest tank for children to use and also one of the most inexpensive is the Kodacraft roll-film tank. Available with either two aprons for 135mm film (to be used when processing the Snapshooter's 126-size film) or one apron for 120-size film. Other easy-loading reel-type tanks include those available from GAF, FR, Jobo, Paterson, and Yankee.

Thermometer. Photo thermometers are available under various brand names: Kodak darkroom thermometer, readings from 10 to 120 F; Capro photo thermometer, mercury column and clear calibration; FR photographic thermometer, readings from 49 to 90 F; Paterson thermometer, readings from 60 to 120 F.

"U"FILM. Available from Hudson Photographic Industries, Inc., Irvington-on-Hudson, N.Y. 10533. Also available from AV distributor; check the Yellow Pages. Frosted acetate is also acceptable and is available from your local art shop.

Wetting agent. To prevent water spots on film, the use of a wetting agent is advisable. Use according to directions. Various brand names include Edwal, FR, Kodak, etc.

Wood stripping. A 1½″ flat moulding available at your local discount lumber supply in lengths of 8′ to 10′.

Write-on slide materials. Kodak Ektagraphic Write-on Slides, available from your local photo dealer.

X-rays. Available from your local radiologist, hospital, or physician.